CASE IN POINT

CRAFTING YOUR CONSULTING CAREER

Insider Insights to Successfully
Navigate Consulting

EVAN PIEKARA

Foreword by Marc P. Cosentino

Case In Point: Crafting Your Consulting Career

ISBN: 978-0-9863707-8-6

Case In Point: Crafting Your Consulting Career by Evan Piekara

Printed in the United States of America

Edited by: Monica Jainschigg

Cover and Interior Layout Design by: Jayme Johnson - Worthy Marketing Group

PRAISE

"*Case In Point: Crafting Your Consulting Career* is a practical guide for anyone considering a career in consulting...read this book – and learn from one of the best." —**Christie Lindor, CEO, Tessi Consulting, professor, and author of** *The MECE Muse: 100+ Selected Practices, Unwritten Rules,* **and** *Habits of Great Consultants*

"This book is a must for those looking to accelerate their careers in consulting. The tips and techniques will allow the reader to hit the ground running, to master techniques across networking, team-building, and skill-building to guarantee long-term success." —**Matt Chambers, Vice President of Education for the Management Consulting Association at UCLA Anderson and new hire at McKinsey & Company**

"Piekara helps you get a front-row seat on how to start, advance, and take your consulting career to the next level. Pure gold!" —**Joe Stimac, CEO and founder of Accuhire.com and Interviewready.com**

"Whether you are an aspiring or current consultant, you will benefit from the anecdotes, interviews, and insights provided by consultants who have labored over key career decisions. Readers will gain an advantage from the lessons learned in this book; it is a must-read to successfully navigate your consulting career!" —**Doreen Amorosa, Associate Dean, Career Services at Georgetown University McDonough School of Business**

"I wish I had had a book like this when I started my career, which answers every single question someone might have about consulting. I am sure that many will benefit from this book and get a jump-start on their career. It is laid out so clearly, and you can tell that the writer is an experienced consultant himself." —**Prerika Agarwal, career empowerment coach and host of the** *Career by Design* **podcast**

"Whether you are a seasoned consultant or just beginning your career as one, look no further than *Case In Point: Crafting Your Consulting Career*. This book is your roadmap for not only succeeding as a consultant and advancing your career, but also making a positive impact on your clients, businesses, and community." —**Eric L. Williamson, author of** *How to Work with Jerks* **and the forthcoming book** *How to Promote a Jerk-Free Environment*

"A must-read for those considering a consulting career, and full of useful advice for seasoned consultants." —**Dolph Goldenburg,** *Successful Nonprofits* **podcast**

"This book expertly showcases the many decisions and career paths for consultants. As someone who has done two ventures in the past, took a sabbatical to pursue my passion for writing, and is currently working on my next idea, I've had to think through many of the critical decisions and how to best leverage my consulting experience. This book would have been a great resource. I highly recommend that all students, budding entrepreneurs, and management consultants read this book."
—**Smarthveer Sidana, associate consultant at Boston Consulting Group**

TABLE OF CONTENTS

III: Building Your Career: Your Next 3-5 Years   151

IV: Life After Consulting

FOREWORD

For the last 30 years, *Case In Point* has been focused on preparing students and industry hires to get jobs in consulting. And for the most part, we've been incredibly successful, sending thousands of people into the top consulting firms across the globe. What we didn't think about was what happens once they get hired. It's a different strategy and mindset once you've entered that world. Even though these firms may have great training programs and provide mentors, people have had to find their own way through the maze of red tape, company politics, and internal competition seemingly alone. Promising consulting careers may have been cut short or not fulfilled to their greatest potential because of uninformed decisions or poor mentorship programs. There wasn't a roadmap or any kind of guidance.

Now there is.

I'm very excited that Evan Piekara has addressed this critical gap with *Case In Point: Crafting Your Consulting Career.* Working on the premise that "no one gets to where they are without help, advice, and support," Evan has developed a comprehensive plan to help you control, design, and get the most out of your career, starting with the simple but brilliant concept of PBA – your personal board of advisors – by building relationships inside the firm and out. He points out what's important, such as angling to get on the right engagement to not only build your skill base but to cultivate your personal brand to maximize your exposure within the firm and thus develop your influence. He helps you craft a 3–5 year plan to help you look at the big picture – *your* big picture – and guides you in thinking through your career goals, the risks involved, and the next steps, both in the short-term and long-term.

You've worked hard to get here. Now take advantage of the ideas and strategies Evan has provided to make the most out of your career.

Marc P. Cosentino
Santa Barbara, California, 2021

1

INTRODUCTION:
SO YOU WANT TO BE A CONSULTANT...

So you want to be a consultant. Whenever I get the inevitable, "So what do you do?" question at events, people are always taken a little aback when I say I'm a consultant. What does that even mean? There are various ways that people "consult," and this profession is prevalent across nearly all industries. When I see the raised eyebrow or look of confusion, I break it down as consultants often do. A consultant is a PPS – *a professional problem solver*. As a PPS, you are brought in to provide an independent perspective on a business problem that an organization is facing. You may leverage particular knowledge, skills, or experiences that the organization does not have in-house, and you likely use this understanding, frameworks, analysis, and a specialized toolkit to help that organization identify, solve, or build a solution for that problem.

Solving challenges is rarely easy. You have to be politically astute, an extremely good listener (to both what is said and unsaid), and able to build relationships to help you get the information you need and to build bridges. Often, you need to get up to speed very quickly on a situation that you know little about; and like a scientist, you build and test assumptions and gather data to evaluate your hypothesis. A consultant needs to be comfortable with ambiguity, be creative while also being process-driven, and be able to think critically about actions and next steps. A consultant must be an effective communicator who is able to present with confidence, synthesize information, and break complex issues down into easily digestible nuggets of information. A consultant must be able to get their message to stick. And if it doesn't stick, they can't wallow in that disappointment – they need to reflect on what lessons they learned for the next project. They are constant learners who seek growth and continuous improvement.

Consultants have to be prepared to put in months of work only to see their recommendations rejected by the client. They have to have a thick skin and know that at times, they'll be the scapegoat for institutional inertia and objectives not fully being met. They have to accept that they own project failures and that the client owns project successes. They have to be ready to be viewed as an unwelcome outsider, a rude intruder, a disruptor. Consultants must also face the very real possibility that as they build partnerships and even friendships with the client, they could be suddenly whisked off, like a free agent, to another team or need. They also need to consider that, like a mercenary, they are hired pay providing an outsourced service to the client and while they may root for client success, they also serve other masters – their project team and firm. This can be the tightest of tightropes to walk.

Consulting is competitive – you compete against other firms for business by building relationships, capturing information, and writing proposal after proposal (thinking and rethinking that graphic, that wording, that value proposition, that solution design) to support your firm. And within your company, you may compete for high-profile projects or to be on a particular team or recruit members to your project team. You compete for promotions, salary, and for personal brand recognition. You compete against yourself, striving for continued growth and improvement. While not all firms have this culture, many do, and I'd say the very nature of consulting attracts collaborative competitors.

Consulting is not always glamorous. It can be long hours, time on the road away from family and friends, and intense pressure. It can be fast food in the airport huddled over your laptop, early-morning coffees after late-night planning sessions, and having to be "on" for extended periods of time. It can strain relationships, test loyalties, and bring out the worst in people. It can also bring out the best in people as you learn, adapt, and connect strengths to solve an insurmountable problem. Consulting means learning another language ("consultant speak" is a thing), always being "on" (where work principles and "best practices" bleed into your personal life), and balancing competing priorities.

So, after all of that, do you still want to be a consultant? This book is a compilation of the most common questions that I have received from aspiring consultants, junior consultants, and managers I have mentored or who have reached out for advice – and it includes some of the biggest decisions that you will need to make as a consultant. This book will help you navigate a consulting career from your earliest considerations, to setting your sails and launching your consulting journey, to exploring new possibilities and opportunities. It will help you evaluate and make those critical decisions at the crossroads of your career and enter consulting with a far better understanding of what you will experience. These lessons learned come from my personal experience and the experience of many other consultants. They paint a picture of the many opportunities, pathways, and decisions you will need to consider as you craft your consulting career. While my experience is just one perspective, I've also included gems of wisdom from nearly 20 consultants who have had to traverse through challenges, opportunities, and critical decision points. No career is an island and no perspective should be taken as doctrine. These perspectives will guide you through the forest and travel your own career path in consulting or beyond. Happy consulting!

HOW TO USE THIS BOOK

One theme that will surface throughout this book is that the path to partner starts before you arrive at your firm. "Partner," however, does not need to be the career-defining moment – and too often, consultants make the mistake of measuring their success by this milestone rather than by what they have learned, how they have grown, and who they have helped along the way. Consulting provides versatile skills and a strong network that can be used across many roles and industries. These skills open many paths and opportunities to build your career. This book is designed to help you manage your consulting career by anticipating and planning for the myriad decisions you will need to make. It is broken down into a high-level life cycle of the typical consulting career and provides insights that apply to the level you're currently at, or aspiring to. This book is a compilation of the nearly 50 most common questions that I have been asked by aspiring consultants and those looking to advance in their consulting careers. It contains lessons I have gained through hard experience, my own mistakes, and reflection on what I could have done better. And it contains insights from the over 200 informational interviews that have been initiated with me and the over 100 informational interviews that I have initiated with consultants throughout my career. This book also contains insights collected from interviews with nearly twenty esteemed consulting professionals.

Crafting Your Consulting Career is divided into four primary sections based on the consulting career life cycle: (1) Planning Your Career, (2) Launching Your Career, (3) Building Your Career, and (4) Life After Consulting. Each section highlights common questions and decisions that you'll face, approaches for evaluating these decisions, and insights and anecdotes from successful consulting professionals. Many decisions will even occur well before you even sign your acceptance letter. You may need to consider which skills to develop, how to craft your resume, whether or not to get an advanced degree. Then, of course, there is which firm, business line, and office are right for you. The projects you support, the knowledge and skills that you build, the network and reputation that you establish all start with the launch of your consulting career. These networks, your reputation, and expertise will enable you to build your career and choose the path or paths that are right for you.

While each section could be a stand-alone, I recommend reading this book cover to cover and then revisiting applicable sections. There are several reasons for this. First, no matter where you are in your career, you should be prepared for the steps it takes to get to the next level and which decisions you will need to make. While the route is seldom linear, it helps to know what to expect at the next level and begin to strive for that level. Second, you will have the opportunity throughout your career to share knowledge and provide mentorship – whether to more junior people, peers, or even managing up. Reflecting on perspectives gained from this book will make you a better mentor. Third, while this book is divided into sections aligned to the stages of your career, it contains considerations and points that may impact you no matter the stage you're at.

Career paths can be circuitous, and being aware of your options can help shape your actions. Whether on the partner track, moving into industry, starting your own company, or taking on another role outside of consulting, you'll need to make critical career decisions to get you there (and to form the networks that help you along the way). Use this book to help you build that roadmap to career success – and please share takeaways with others.

PLANNING YOUR CONSULTING CAREER

How do you build your resume for consulting? Whom should you seek out for advice? Which firm, business line, or office is right for you? How do you build a plan for the future? Consultants apply strategic planning and critical thinking skills to solve complex business problems for organizations, and these competencies can be scaled across your career. Planning your career starts with creating a roadmap and examining the prospective paths you can take. Advance awareness of these paths enables you to make it less perilous, to prioritize the direction you want to go, and to determine potential crossroads where you may want to pivot or adjust course. Take time to climb the tree and survey the forest before blindly walking into the woods.

Planning your career is an activity that you should not do alone. Build and use your network – reach out to alumni; ask established contacts for introductions; and learn from the various tools, resources, and thought leaders sharing their knowledge. The path to partner, industry executive, social-sector leader, or entrepreneur begins with careful planning, and reading this section will help you progress more quickly and take a less circuitous route to your chosen goal. That said, recognize that priorities shift, opportunities arise, and the unexpected happens, and you may have to change your plans. A recurring theme will be that career paths are rarely linear, and no matter which stage you're at in your career, this section will help you make decisions that could impact your future. Use it to help you build the agility you need to adapt your plans in support of your career.

1

WHO SHOULD BE ON YOUR PERSONAL BOARD OF ADVISORS?

I received one of the best pieces of advice during my senior year of college. Little did I know that I was about to jump-start my career on the precipice of the Great Recession and would need to navigate uncertainty, be flexible in searching for job opportunities, and find ways to differentiate and re-create myself during a time when I was still figuring out my career path. This life-altering advice was to form my own "personal board of advisors" (PBA). Just as companies and nonprofits bring together people with diverse networks, backgrounds, and expertise to hold them accountable and guide their actions, a PBA can do the same for you, drawing together distinct people who are willing to offer advice, talk through experiences, and share unvarnished feedback. I've built a PBA for several aspects of my life – career, community, and as a new parent. PBAs have guided me in evaluating decisions that have shaped my life:

- Should I join Teach For America?
- Do I need an advanced degree? If so, what degree should I get?
- Where should I get my MBA?
- What career best suits me?
- Which company can I best contribute to?

PBAs have also held me accountable for:

- Writing *Case In Point: Government and Nonprofit* and this book
- Joining and actively leading nonprofit boards
- Designing workshops and opportunities that share knowledge
- Making it a priority to share my time with the community and provide mentoring to others

As a new parent, I've started building a PBA for more than just career and community. This "Family PBA" has helped me adapt to becoming a father during the coronavirus and to learn how to be the best father I can be.

Building a PBA requires intentionality, commitment, and adaptability. It necessitates regular maintenance by earning and building trust and confidence, and continuing to show a deep appreciation for those who are willing to help you on your path.

No one gets to where they are without help, advice, and support. Here's how to build the PBA that will provide them.

BE INTENTIONAL

Whenever I face a major life decision, am evaluating opportunities, or need someone to hold me accountable, I reach out to individuals on my PBA. I'll share my considerations, concerns, and potential paths and listen to their insights and feedback. Often, this has helped me sharpen my focus and make better decisions.

A PBA is five to seven people who know you, want to see you succeed, and have your trust. Not everyone you know ticks these boxes – and you may find that very few people do. You have to invest in building these relationships, actively seeking out peers and mentors who are willing to share their experiences, offer guidance, and help you evaluate decisions. Note that I said "peers" as well as "mentors." Because these are people who may be experiencing similar circumstances or who are at similar stages in their careers, it's valuable to have their perspective as well. Sharing with an inner circle of peers whom you trust can also lead to more open, casual conversations, and provides a safer place to test ideas, voice doubts, and talk through concerns. And particularly as you advance in your career, it's also important to consider having some junior colleagues serve on your PBA so that you can capture feedback from all levels of your team. Having an array of experiences and perspectives can help you identify blind spots and mind the gaps.

As I prepared to launch my career, my initial PBA consisted of a professor who served as my advisor, a close career-minded friend, a friend and confidant who helped me strategize steps and review decisions, a business executive who had mentored me during my internship the previous summer, and my undergraduate college president, who had initially imparted the wisdom of having a PBA to me. These five people helped me choose a path and would be guides whenever I reached a fork in the road.

Don't be afraid to be vulnerable with these people by sharing your concerns and fears, accepting their straightforward feedback, and keeping them updated on your decisions, progress, and life changes. As you build your PBA, consider:

- Where do I need the greatest support?
- Where are my biggest gaps? Who might help me discover things that I am not even aware that I do not know?
- Who are the people in my corner – people who want me to succeed? How do I know?
- Who would I like to have in my corner? How do I get them there?
- What knowledge, skills, and experiences would help me advance in my career?
- How can I build trust with this group?
- How can I support this group?

Part of being intentional is actively building and maintaining relationships. It is determining which objective this group will serve and what problems this group will help you address. It is also being aware of where you fall short, what gaps you have, and how someone else's advice and experience can help you overcome those gaps. Perhaps, most importantly, it is recognizing that you must also be there for your PBA and actively find ways to support them as well.

BE COMMITTED

A PBA requires commitment. This means you do not just reach out whenever you have an issue that you want to talk through. Like a garden, you must plant the seed of the relationship in the right soil, tend to it regularly by removing weeds and debris (for instance, people who may not have your best interests in mind, may not provide the right expertise, or may not be able to commit the time) and ensuring that it has adequate sunlight and water (your support, contribution, and presence), and, at times, you might prune it. Don't just "set and forget" your PBA. Make sure to provide regular updates on your life and career, send spontaneous thank-you notes and acknowledgments of the role that they have played in your career, and celebrate their successes along with them. PBA relationships are often long-term, and their members are invested in your success. Give them a reason to be invested – show appreciation for their time, recognize the role they played in your accomplishments, and help them achieve as well.

BE ADAPTABLE

Just as the goals or strategy of an organization may shift, your strategy may change as well. Just as boards have term limits and may recruit new members to provide an area of expertise to address the challenge at hand, your PBA may evolve over time. And while you should continue to maintain contact with those who helped you get to where you are, you should also continue to evolve your PBA. New members may contribute with more specialized experience and insights. You may need to build distinct PBAs with a specific goal in mind (for instance, my creation of a Family PBA). As your goals and priorities change, make sure you are reviewing your PBA(s) and building one that aligns with those goals and priorities, adding members who can help you reach your goals.

Shelley Rappaport is a consultant who has served on my PBA at times (whether knowingly or unknowingly). She has had an extensive 20-plus-year career in consulting and has built expertise around performance management, strategic planning, and change management. Her career has run the gamut – from small boutique firm, to growing leviathan firm, to consulting think tank, to independent consultant, to scrappy entrepreneurial firm. Shelley and I teamed on a project during a formative stage in my consulting career, and her experience helped me learn, grow, and evaluate my choices. She provided unadorned guidance at various stages of my career and when I struggled with seemingly complicated company, client, and broader consulting industry challenges.

When I asked her about the most important piece of advice for consultants planning and launching their career, she responded without hesitation:

> Find a mentor. It doesn't even have to be someone you work with or who is even part of your same company. Make sure this person is someone who you can connect with and who shares your values. One of my first bosses is this person for me, and nearly 20 years later, I still call her up for advice. This relationship does not have to be overly formal. Find people who are willing to ask questions, listen, and help you think through what is best for you and your career.

When you find people like Shelley, make sure to keep in touch!

While you can certainly succeed without a PBA, having these regular advisory sessions can instill confidence, incorporate feedback, and craft a better career.

2

HOW DO YOU POSITION YOURSELF TO ENTER CONSULTING?

Not everyone takes a straight route to a consulting career. Many consultants made the switch from a very different path. Similar approaches and tools can be used for trying to enter consulting from undergraduate or as someone who is switching careers. Launching your career with limited experience or leaving the comfort of a career you know well can be daunting. You may second-guess yourself, fear that you lack the knowledge and skills to succeed in a new opportunity, and wonder if anyone would be willing to take a chance on you. Countless people have reached out to me on LinkedIn or come across the article "Teacher Turned Management Consultant Shares Career Change Tips"[1] and wanted to learn how I made the jump from sixth- and seventh-grade English and history teacher in the South Bronx to management consultant. Firms are looking for people who are client-ready, and those looking to build a bridge to a consulting career can show client readiness by: (1) understanding the role, (2) explicitly showing transferable skills, (3) building analogies.

UNDERSTANDING THE ROLE

If you've made it past the introduction, then you are already addressing the first step by better understanding the role of a consultant. Remember the idea of the professional problem-solver? When hiring a PPS, most firms look for five core skills:

- **Communication:** Are you able to clearly articulate and get your message across?
- **Critical Thinking (Analytics):** Do you connect the dots? Are you able to consider qualitative and quantitative factors in thinking through a problem?
- **Leadership:** Do you show initiative? Are you able to influence or

motivate a group?

- **Project Management:** Do you get things done? Are you able to prioritize?
- **Teamwork:** Are you collaborative? Do you apply or adapt your skills to support the team?

Teaching was far and away the hardest job I have ever had. It was long hours presenting material to the fiercest critics (sixth-graders can be brutal and are not afraid to give you unsolicited feedback). It was figuring out where each student was starting and determining how to best guide and motivate them to achieve distant goals. It was looking at 185 school days, recognizing that there would be vacations, field trips, sick days, test days, and other disruptions, and trying to align my curriculum to ensure key learning milestones were achieved in that time frame. It was building a culture that supported students, enabled them to be vulnerable, and helped them to achieve. Teachers do not get enough credit for what they do, and I commend anyone who has spent time teaching (and great teachers certainly deserve higher pay!). After four years in the classroom, I sought to have an impact on a more systemic level by helping mission-oriented organizations develop and design sustainable solutions to pervasive problems. Consulting was one avenue to achieve this.

I started by understanding what a consultant did. Reading books like Marc Cosentino's *Case In Point* helped provide a baseline understanding, and I found conversations with actual consultants were the best way to pick up their language, see how they presented themselves, and learn what their day-to-day was like. Hearing about consultants from consultants in their own words helped me begin to see how my skill set as a teacher applied beyond the classroom.

EXPLICITLY SHOWING TRANSFERABLE SKILLS

Explicitly is emphasized for a reason. Too often, recruiters, firms, and people in our networks might write off career-switchers or those with limited consulting experience. When I was seeking my first consulting job, many recruiters failed to see the immediate parallel between teaching and consulting. They created a narrative that these two roles were so entirely different that I could not possibly make a good consultant. Don't let them create this narrative! Better yet, you create the narrative. You can build on your understanding of what a consultant does by showing that you are already demonstrating consulting skills. Highlight these in your resume and align them with consulting position descriptions. Quantify your resume bullets to show results. When people are building their resumes or trying to switch careers, I always suggest two things: (1) STAR format, and (2) a skills-based resume.

STAR stands for situation, task, action, results. A STAR format helps you tell a story that showcases what you were doing, which skills or actions you used, and your (quantified, when possible) impact. With the skills-based resume, I recommend explicitly starting your bullet with the corresponding consulting skill that you want to showcase and then using the STAR format to expand on it. Knowing that communication is a critical consulting skill and that this was a skill that every teacher uses daily, a bullet on my resume might look like:

- **Communication:** Facilitated over 4,000 hours of sessions by designing presentations, activities, and individualized and group exercises breaking complex knowledge and skills into core components, resulting in 120+ learners meeting 95% of objectives within 185 days, exceeding target by 15%.

There's a lot to unpack in this bullet, but it shows a number of things – that I can command a room and facilitate when needed, that I can communicate and break down complex information, and that I can set goals and drive a group toward achieving them. Starting to sound like a consultant?

BUILDING ANALOGIES

Moving from a different career to a consulting career becomes much less perilous when you use analogies to bridge between what you are currently doing to what you will be doing as a consultant. The key is to show that you already have the skills and have been operating as a consultant in your current role(s). For example, the resume example above took teaching responsibilities and put them in the context of a consulting skill – communication. Education jargon was removed, and accomplishments quantified to show results and impact. Build stories that show how you are employing consulting skills in your current role (or if in college, in your courses and student organizations). Use these stories to show that you are already thinking like a consultant, are using consulting skills, and have an understanding of what will be expected of you.

As a teacher, I had to develop a plan to get my students from start to finish.

There were a certain number of units that we needed to cover, quizzes and tests to ensure that students were learning effectively, and times when I would need to adjust course because of an unexpected event – an assembly, a snow day, a lesson that needed to be taught better. On its face, this does not sound like consulting, but in fact it employs the very same skills.

Let's look at this another way: Just as a consultant would do, I built a long-term project plan to cover the next 185 business days. When designing this plan, I established regular objectives, milestones, and checkpoints to evaluate and assess our progress against our goals and targets. If a goal was not met, I would review where we fell short, adapt our timeline, and identify opportunities to ensure that we met our goal. Given our tight time constraints and the fact that our team often had different skill sets and strengths, I often had to develop individualized and group approaches to help us achieve our goal. Over the course of these 185 days, we built a strong culture of learning and continuous improvement, and while our initial target was 80%, we were able to achieve 95% of our learning objectives.

Putting your story in the language of a consultant and likening it to consulting paints the relevance of your experience. Whatever path you come from, you can help build a bridge for your interview by showcasing that you are already using consulting skills. Again, teaching was far and away the hardest thing I have ever done (and this includes consulting). But when I made the switch to consulting, I had to convince myself and others that I had the needed skills and did this by crafting a narrative and aligning my stories and experiences to what a consultant does. By demonstrating that you understand the role, have the skills for the role, and are already applying those skills, you open the door to an offer.

3

HOW DO YOU BUILD YOUR CONSULTING RESUME?

When you look at everything with a consulting project lens, then you can easily build your resume with this sharpened focus. As I shared in the previous chapter, you can use understanding of the consultant's role, transferable skills, and analogies to show that you are doing "consulting," just in a different context. Reframe your current experiences. Are you volunteering for an organization? Are you involved in or leading an extracurricular club? Are you taking a course that requires analysis, critical thinking, and problem-solving? If none of these experiences apply right now, you can start finding ways to build that resume.

VOLUNTEER!

We volunteer to give back to our communities, help others, be grateful for what we have, and to feel good. One often overlooked opportunity is to volunteer in order to develop skills and build your resume. Countless nonprofits are looking for regular volunteers who are able to share their time and talents. Many may even offer training to volunteers who make a long-term commitment. Moreover, organizations like DoSomething, VolunteerMatch, boardnetUSA, Idealist, Compass, and the Taproot Foundation (to name a few) offer databases of skills-based volunteer opportunities and structured consulting projects.

What does volunteering signal? It shows that you are managing your time to be an active and engaged member of your community (and suggests that you will be an active and engaged member of your company). It demonstrates a willingness to use your time and talents for others (and this translates well into being a great teammate). Volunteering also shows a desire to better yourself and those around you (continuous improvement).

As you become more embedded and a more regular volunteer for the organization, you may even be able to identify business challenges that you could help the organization solve and have this become a "consulting project."

When I was a first-year teacher as part of Teach For America, there was a stretch during the first few months when morale was low for me and many of my closest corps-member friends. We were working long hours, struggling to meet our goals, and losing that personal connection and sense of camaraderie that we had experienced during our institute training. A group of us self-organized and began to assess why we were facing these challenges and the impact morale had on student achievement and teacher retention – two strategic metrics important to TFA. While a lot of our observations were anecdotal, we were able to capture testimonials, institute our own survey to capture quantitative data, and develop a plan. We connected with TFA leaders, and, to their credit, they were very receptive to our findings and collaborated with us on an effort to boost morale and reinvigorate our corps. When I ultimately applied to business school, this example of volunteering became a prime component of my application and provided me with a "consulting project" to showcase on my resume.

RELEVANT COURSEWORK

In the previous chapter, I highlighted some core consulting skills (communication, critical thinking, project management, teamwork, and leadership). Do any of these skills resonate with you? Would you consider any to be strengths? Are there some gaps where you have limited or no proficiency? Consultants are lifelong learners who continuously seek to build their knowledge and skills. Signal this on your resume with relevant coursework. Target courses that will build relevant skills and fill in those gaps in your resume. Identify core capabilities that you want to develop or strengthen, map these courses in the bevy of online options for ongoing learning (LinkedIn Learning, General Assembly), and invest time in taking these courses to support your entrance into consulting and ongoing career growth. Create a relevant coursework or ongoing learning section on your resume to highlight the courses you've taken.

EXTRACURRICULAR ACTIVITIES

Extracurricular activities are not only a great way to pursue your passions, grow your network, and develop skills, but also are an opportunity to make a connection with the interviewer or tell a story. Like volunteering, extracurriculars signal a desire to connect with your community (company), ability to prioritize and manage time, and that you're continuing to build or demonstrate skills. Even something as seemingly trivial as joining an intramural basketball league can showcase teamwork and leadership skills.

One extracurricular that I always recommend is Toastmasters International (https://www.toastmasters.org/). For those unfamiliar with Toastmasters, it is a group that meets regularly (typically twice a month for an hour and a half) to develop their leadership and public speaking skills. Attendees perform roles such as moderating and leading the meeting, being a speaker giving a five- to seven-minute speech or presentation to the group, and being an evaluator who provides feedback to the speaker(s).

Toastmasters is relatively inexpensive, full of valuable resources, and has easily accessible groups all over the world. This organization is a phenomenal way to build leadership skills, hone your public speaking and presentation skills, and get out of your comfort zone – all things consultants should demonstrate. There is even a section of the meeting designated for someone to speak extemporaneously on a topic for one to two minutes (you definitely need to be quick on your feet as a consultant!). It is also a great way to learn and develop your feedback muscles in both giving and receiving feedback. These meetings also double as valuable networking opportunities – I've made some good friends and met very interesting people through Toastmasters.

These skills and experiences translate extremely well into consulting and enable you to make a very direct case for how you are developing your communication and leadership skills, managing your time and meetings, and taking the initiative. If there is not a group in your locality, you can easily create one (what a great way to show initiative, leadership skills, and project management)!

****

Don't take all of these tips at once – it's quality over quantity. Prioritize your time and what skills you build and show on your resume. Being a committed volunteer or Toastmaster will go much further than only attending a few volunteer sessions or meetings. Make sure you are being intentional with your time, the skills that you are building, and the story that you want to tell.

4

WHAT MEDIA RESOURCES CAN HELP YOU SHARPEN YOUR KNOWLEDGE?

Social media is a powerful tool that can help you stay informed, build your knowledge, and make connections. While networking and coffee chats can lead to valuable perspective on companies and the industry, checking quick snapshots from Twitter, reviews and articles, newspaper headlines, and podcasts can keep you learning.

PODCASTS

It's not always easy to prepare for a career in consulting during your commute, while at the gym, or while running errands. Podcasts help you prepare for consulting while on the go. There are a number of podcasts that can help you to better understand complex business problems, hear creative solutions that can be modified for other industries, or simply just show that curiosity and love of learning that many consulting companies are looking for. Below are some of the most useful podcasts and resources that I have found for learning and preparing for consulting.

General Business Podcasts. Here is a selection of three business podcasts that cover an array of topics from organizational design to marketing, workforce development, and management.

- **Harvard Business Review (HBR) IdeaCast (https://hbr.org/2018/01/podcast-ideacast):** At nearly 700 episodes on a broad range of topics, the Ideacast provides greater context on many of HBR's articles in quick 10- to 30-minute episodes.
- **Six Pixels of Separation (https://www.sixpixels.com/):** This podcast provides insights into branding, marketing, social media, technology, and how connected we all have become.
- **WorkLife (https://www.ted.com/podcasts/worklife):** On this podcast, organizational psychologist and Wharton professor Adam

Grant provides thoughtful ideas and insights on how to improve the work environment.

I'll add a bonus podcast (full disclosure, I serve as an advisor for this company). vCoach Academy is an India-based company established by Boston Consulting Group alumni. They have been putting out some excellent podcast content on a range of topics, including interviews with consultants and industry thought leaders. These short podcasts are packed with thought-provoking information.

Government Podcasts. The three podcasts I've listed below will help you better understand the unique challenges and opportunities that the government faces. These conversations with industry experts with real-world experience will give you some case studies, frameworks, and broaden your thinking on government solutions.

- **The Business of Government Radio Hour (https://www. podcastone.com/the-business-of-government-hour):** Put on by the IBM Center for Business and Government, this is a weekly podcast with each episode clocking in at nearly an hour. The shows are packed with interviews, case studies, and information about how agencies and their leaders are leading strategy and transformation efforts.
- **Gov Innovator (https://govinnovator.com/):** This podcast has nearly 200 episodes and covers state and local as well as federal topics. Interviews with industry leaders provide real-world case studies and insights on government innovations.
- **GovLove (https://elgl.org/govlove/):** This podcast focuses on the people, policies, and profession of those in local government, providing unique insights and case studies on a much more localized level.

Nonprofit Podcasts. The nonprofit industry faces its own distinct opportunities and challenges as these organizations try to meet their mission and increase their impact. Here are three podcasts to help you prepare for the industry.

- **The Business of Giving (https://denver-frederick.com/):** This weekly, hourlong podcast is hosted by Denver Frederick, who has 40-plus years of experience in the philanthropy world. It explores possible solutions to today's social problems, including global poverty, affordable housing, clean drinking water, and education.

- **Stanford Social Innovation Review Inside Social Innovation (https://ssir.org/podcasts):** The SSIR podcast comprises conversations with leading experts on social entrepreneurship and innovation, and covers specific case studies within the social sector. Initially, it also covers topics such as mergers and acquisitions in the nonprofit space as well as diversity, equity, and inclusion.
- **Successful Nonprofits (https://successfulnonprofits.com/):** This podcast covers opportunities that many nonprofits face, including managing risk, developing a fundraising strategy, and leveraging social media. This is my favorite podcast – the topics cut across many industries and often provide best practices beyond just nonprofit; the host is warm and engaging; and the interviews are fascinating. (I really enjoyed my time on Successful Nonprofits (shameless plug), https://successfulnonprofits.com/portfolio/job_interviews_piekera/.)

TWITTER AND NEWSLETTERS

Along with regularly listening to the podcasts you like, I'd recommend making it a habit to scan the headlines of newsletters and Twitter. I regularly scroll Twitter for headlines and thought leadership pieces to get a sense for what people are saying. Here are some worthwhile Twitter pages to follow.

For general business, I recommend following on Twitter Adam Grant (@AdamMGrant), Reuters Business (@ReutersBiz), the *Wall Street Journal Business News* (@WSJbusiness), *Fortune* (@fortunemagazine), *Business Insider* (@businessinsider), and Johnny C. Taylor, the CEO of the Society for Human Resource Management (@JohnnyCTaylorJr). The one that I probably review the most often is the *Harvard Business Review* (@HarvardBiz). For newsletters, I'd recommend the Harvard Business Review Management Tip of the Day, which provides concise, topical management best practices, and the 1440 Daily Digest, which consolidates the hottest news stories of the day into quick summaries with links to the articles for more information.

For news from the public sector, I'd follow on Twitter McKinsey on Government (@McKonGov), LawFare (@lawfareblog), Government Business Council (@GovExecInsights), *Federal Times* (@FederalTimes), and the Federal News Network (@FederalNewsNetwork). GovExec also puts out a great daily newsletter.

For nonprofit updates on Twitter, I'd recommend The Bridgespan Group (@BridgespanGroup), *Nonprofit Quarterly* (@NonprofitQuarterly),

Dolph Goldenburg (@DolphGoldenburg), Inside Philanthropy (@ InsidePhilanthr), Nonprofit Daily (@nonprofitdaily), Philanthropy Daily (@philanthropydaily), and Anand Gridharadas (@Anandwrites). The *Nonprofit Quarterly* and *Stanford Social* Innovation Review also have fantastic newsletters.

5

DO YOU NEED AN ADVANCED DEGREE?

D o you need an advanced degree? It depends. Add this phrase to your consulting repertoire! Seldom are answers as simple as "yes" or "no." As a consultant, you find a way to structure problems, evaluate options, and determine the approach that best fits the situation. There is no cookie-cutter, one-size-fits-all answer, and a question, like any consulting problem, involves building a framework, evaluating and weighting factors, and determining what makes sense given your unique situation. When evaluating this question, I'd consider (1) individual/internal factors (IIFs) and (2) environmental/external factors (EEFs).

INDIVIDUAL/INTERNAL FACTORS

Individual/internal factors (IIFs) are considerations that are more personal to you and may impact your ability to earn an advanced degree. As you decide whether to pursue an advanced degree, you want to consider things such as:

- **Time:** Can I dedicate approximately two years to earning an advanced degree? While there are flexible programs (programs have been creating more flexible options that include longer timelines and condensed versions to accommodate different lifestyles), you are most likely committing to two years of intensive learning.
- **Cost:** Do I have the ability to finance through loans and rely on savings or other income while I earn my degree? Am I willing to take a mortgage on myself? You're likely looking at 10 years or more of paying back your loan.
- **Opportunity Cost:** What else could I be doing with my time and money during this time, and would earning an advanced degree be a better use of my time? Opportunity cost is an extremely important concept that most fail to factor into their decision. Consider your current role and earnings potential and whether or not an advanced degree would enable you to substantially increase that earnings potential over that time and if

there are ways to get to your goal without an advanced degree.
- **Social Considerations:** Am I willing to relocate? Am I willing to have limited time with family and friends and commit to getting this degree? Can I and those impacted by this decision adapt?

When I was evaluating whether or not to get an advanced degree, I looked at these IIFs and began developing a 3–5 year roadmap. From a social consideration standpoint, I was in my mid-twenties, living in New York City, and single. My decision did not really affect anyone beyond me. No one would have to relocate, I had no children, or no one else had to adjust to a demanding schedule while I earned my degree. I could dedicate the time without putting an added burden on someone else.

As a teacher in New York, I had little savings, and there were undergraduate student loans that I was still paying off. And higher education, as we know, is not cheap. I was going to be looking at close to $200,000, which I could finance through loans and pay back over the next decade or so. Taking out a loan like this is a personal mortgage, and it can be a "crossing the Rubicon" moment when you are truly investing in, and betting on, yourself. You've got better information that anyone on whether or not it's a good bet to make. I evaluated whether I would be better off continuing to teach for two years in New York or using these two years to build a path to another career, and how each of these options would contribute to my long-term earnings potential.

At the time, I was earning approximately $56,000 a year and would receive a modest salary increase each year. As a career switcher, even if I used those two years to build my network and skills and transition into consulting, I felt that I would only moderately increase my earnings potential and would still lack core skills and credibility to advance rapidly in an organization. Most starting MBA salaries were double what I was currently earning, with signing bonuses, anticipated pay increases, and year-end bonuses adding to the total compensation. From a time and cost standpoint, my decision to invest in a degree, while initially overwhelming, started to crystallize. From an earnings potential standpoint, it made more sense. There was also little consequence to friends or family. So as a constant learner and believer in the transformative power of education, I set earning an MBA as a personal goal. But before fully committing to this critical choice, I wanted to evaluate the market to ensure that I was not missing anything.

ENVIRONMENTAL/EXTERNAL FACTORS

While IIFs are directly within your locus of control, many more will be beyond your power. Environmental/external factors (EEFs) may be difficult to forecast, but many advanced degree publications and programs will provide market research to help you better assess these EEFs. For instance, you may want to consider:

- **Applicant Pool:** Who is applying to your target schools? Are you meeting the school's published targets (GPA, test scores)? This could impact which schools you apply to, when you apply, and how you differentiate yourself. I always advise applicants that they are far more than their GPA and test scores and that strong recommendations, experience, and essays can also tip admittance in your favor.
- **Applicant Trends:** Have applications been trending up or down over the last few years? What appears to be the demand for a particular degree? These market factors could suggest the degree you choose to pursue. If the degree you initially considered is on the downward trajectory, you might consider whether another specialization is more encompassing or whether a certificate or different program might suffice.
- **Economic Factors:** How is the economy? What is the job market? There was a flood of applicants during and immediately preceding the Great Recession as people opted to get degrees during a period of unemployment and uncertainty. What is the economic forecast, and how could this impact applications?
- **Job Prospects and Trajectory:** What is the average salary from someone coming out of these programs? What is the average salary for roles that you are targeting post-graduation? Does this industry seem to be moving in a positive direction? How does this compare to your current salary and earnings potential?

These were all factors that I considered as I applied to business schools in the wake of the Great Recession. While there was still uncertainty, the market seemed poised for a rebound, so I would be entering a stronger economy with greater job opportunities. While there were more applicants, making the process very competitive, it also enabled me to target a mix of schools to maximize my options and enabled me to look at the "typical" candidate and try to find ways to differentiate myself.

I posed the question of whether or not to pursue an advanced degree to Rohit Agarwal, a TFA alumnus who went to Northwestern's Kellogg School of

Business and rose through McKinsey's ranks to become a senior engagement manager. Rohit would eventually step into an entrepreneurship role before becoming Head of the United States at Kiva. Rohit's is just one opinion, but a valuable one, particularly if you are switching careers:

> I don't like saying yes, but I will say yes. I think there are very few analyst spots at most consulting firms and a high volume of people applying to them. I think it is much easier if you get an MBA because the business schools have a more formalized process with the consulting firms. That being said, it is possible to transition without an MBA! As a teacher, you need to motivate, plan, and execute, which is a vital part of consulting. I think you can build a bridge highlighting transferable skills, but it will take time and networking, and you may have gaps that could be filled with an advanced degree.

****

As you can see, a graduate degree is not a necessity to get into consulting and it is not a decision that you should come to lightly. You will incur long-term debt and the opportunity cost of lost time, and it will be a career crossroads. You may be able to develop a roadmap you can follow to succeed in consulting without an advanced degree (and countless have). Evaluate an advanced degree as part of your overall strategy and consider whether it is the best option in helping you build your skills, expand your network, and capture the credibility to enter the consulting world.

6

HOW DO YOU IDENTIFY A FIRM THAT IS THE RIGHT FIT?

"What *truly* sets us apart is our people!" I attended at least 50 employer presentations in business school with an array of firms and companies sharing more about their firm, what makes it great, and why you should work there. Undoubtedly, someone would ask what sets the firm apart. Almost every firm gave some variation of "Our people!" These firms must all have had phenomenal recruiters and hiring managers! Determining whether a firm is a good fit for you goes beyond just the values listed on their website. It takes (1) knowing your own strengths, (2) having real conversations about the culture of the company, and (3) evaluating what is most important to you.

KNOW YOUR STRENGTHS

Do you love networking? Are you a connector? Do you thrive in environments where you can initiate opportunities, or do you prefer a more structured path? Know what you are good at and see which consulting firms cater to your strengths. If you are a natural networker who is able to map out connections and build strong relationships, then look for firms where networking goes beyond an expectation. You can evaluate this by learning what it takes to be staffed on a project (does a partner or project manager assign you or recruit/request you (networking!) or are you staffed automatically based on openings, forecast, and your skills?). If networking is not something you enjoy, then consider a firm that has a more structured way of staffing you on projects. Or get more comfortable doing something you don't consider a strength.

Firms will share all sorts of initiatives. Do you prefer to join an initiative and add to it, or shape it? When a firm says that they are "entrepreneurial," does that mean that you have to wade through layers of bureaucracy and justifications to get approval for an idea before the firm will provide resources to support it, or is it as simple as presenting a business case to a manager? Some firms will want you to build on the structures already in place, other firms will welcome you helping them build a structure. Determine which one works for you.

Once you identify your three to five core strengths, then you can assess these in real conversations with members of the firm.

HAVE REAL CONVERSATIONS

Real conversations are authentic conversations. These are not the ones that take place during recruiting presentations, at sponsored events, and when everyone is singing the praises of the firm. These are the exchanges where someone may share that the best thing about the firm is not actually the people. That the firm's stated values of work-life balance really translates into 40 to 50 billable hours a week, a set metric where you need to contribute to $X million in business development initiatives on top of your billable hours, and a host of "optional" events that you're encouraged (read, *required*) to attend if you'd like to get a good performance review and be considered for promotion.

Real conversations are unlikely to take place at sponsored or recruiting events where everyone drank the Kool-Aid to pump themselves up prior to arrival. They are the informal "get-to-know-you" conversations that you set up through your network, or even through LinkedIn (*Note:* Try to get an introduction from a mutual connection or reach out to someone within your existing alumni network before cold messaging). These are the chats where you're taking the role of a learner who wants to better understand consulting and the firm's dynamics, and your contact is sharing their words of wisdom. They occur over the comfort and confines of a coffee shop, are often short (20 minutes or so), and where the drink is a cup of coffee, not a gulp of company Kool-Aid. These conversations are also off-the-record, where your connection can share information without worrying that a partner will overhear.

I've been on both sides of these conversations. I'd estimate that I initiated (i.e., as a "learner") nearly 100 (doing the math, this is close to 30 hours of coffee chats) and responded to nearly 200 requests to have such a discussion (I'm generous with my time and would probably put this at close to 100 hours). These conversations are good practice for not only entering the consulting world, but also advancing in your consulting career and beyond.

You can build connections and learn subtle and not-so-subtle tells of when someone is being inauthentic. In the authentic conversations, you might get answers that help you to better evaluate the firm and how it relates to your strengths.

You might hear that someone "had to learn to network" because if they did not "network onto a project," then they ran the risk of a poor review. You might learn that it took three months to get approval to host a women's empowerment initiative or that it simply took a supervisor saying, "Great initiative. I absolutely support it. Just send me a plan and budget, and I'll approve." These are the nuggets that help you to truly evaluate whether or not a firm is the right fit for you.

EVALUATE WHAT IS IMPORTANT TO YOU

Not all consulting firms are created equal, and the bells and whistles that one firm showcases may not be as important to you as other factors. When you are evaluating a firm, you should assess these features against your strengths and further qualify them during your real conversations:

- **Brand:** How does the firm market itself? What is its reputation? What is its place in the market? Some of us are clearly more brand-conscious than others. Do you want the designer label, or are you just as comfortable in something more off-brand? Do you want something more established or something young and scrappy? Brand can bestow credibility on the employee and open doors down the road. This is worth evaluating as part of your long-term consulting strategy.
- **Culture:** Is the firm collaborative or competitive? Is there an up-or-out system (i.e., if you are not advancing or hitting certain metrics, do you plateau or possibly get fired)? Are people looking over their shoulders? Know which environment you thrive in and whether or not you are someone who gets galvanized to greatness by keeping pace with others or if you prefer to run with a pack. Is the firm a partnership, and is partner something you might aspire to? Only a limited number of people can make partner. Consider how you do your best work and whether this firm matches it.
- **Learning/Training:** How important is learning and growth to you? What opportunities does the firm provide for training, certifications, and professional development? Some firms have developed world-class institutions led by in-house trainers and thought leaders and provide a menu of options to choose from in order to further develop your craft.

Others may just provide a stipend and the flexibility to choose your own learning adventure. Consider which you prefer and how either of these options helps you to advance professionally.

- **Network:** What is the firm's retention rate? Where do people go once they leave? What opportunities exist for people to network both within and beyond the company? What is the perception by outsiders of people who work there? Does the firm have a structured way of keeping in touch with people who have gone on to other things (i.e., an alumni network)? Such a network contributes to your and the firm's brand because consulting is also inherently a people business where your network is part of your net worth. Consider how the firm can help you advance both within the firm and beyond.

- **Salary/Compensation/Benefits:** What is the salary relative to other companies? What is the bonus structure? What benefits are offered? But put these in context. As you can see from this list, money isn't everything. In fact, it can often be a red herring. When the firm says "unlimited vacation time," is this really a way of enforcing billable targets and not compensating you for vacation that you are unable to use? When you evaluate salary, compensation, and benefits, consider this as part of the full package that comes along with the firm. A lower salary where you are working an average of 50 hours a week with flexible vacation time might come out to a far higher average hourly rate than a higher salary where the expectation is that you will be on the road, pushing 70 to 80 hours a week.

- **Trajectory:** What is the career track? How long does it typically take to get promoted? What factors does the firm consider when making promotions? Is it a partnership model? What opportunities exist to advance and network within the firm? Career trajectory can play an important role in where you want to work. Knowing what the expectations are, what it takes to advance, and your own timeline for advancing can help you find the firm that is right for this stage in your career (and potentially the long term).

- **Work-Life Balance:** Does the firm expect your work and life to become inseparable? Do they expect you to work nights and weekends to get the job done? Are people taking calls and responding to email while "on vacation"? Time is your scarcest and most precious commodity. Consider what time commitment you are making at various stages of the consulting career life cycle. Does the firm actively help manage burnout, or are people encouraged to push through with performance structures that incentivize it? While personal time may not be your most heavily weighted factor, it is one that you must consider, and its priority could change at various stages in your career.

When I was looking at firms, attending the bevy of employee presentations, and engaging in coffee chats, these were some of the factors that I considered. Post business school, I was still single, and so while salary, brand, and many of these factors were important, I prioritized trajectory, culture, and work-life balance. Thankfully, some of my target firms did not extend an offer, and some real conversations helped me self-select out of others. Narrowing my list, I prioritized an opportunity at a growing firm with a solid brand that was building a management consulting practice. This enabled me to step onto a solid career trajectory with an opportunity to get on the partner track and build a team and culture. The practice I joined emphasized work-life balance and creating a "different kind of consulting company." Because it was still building its infrastructure around training and developing its consulting brand, it gave me the chance to support marketing and drive internal processes – opportunities that I would not have had at other firms. As life changes occurred (getting married, starting a family), some of my priorities shifted as well. This is why it's important to set a 3–5 year plan and continue to revisit your priorities. As your priorities shift, your career path may shift along with it.

When I asked Yashomati Bachul Koul, who has spent over eight years at Kearney and risen to the ranks of principal, about how to identify the right firm for you, they shared,

> I went back to business school after the financial crisis of 2008 forced me to hit "reset" on my career. I was already in my 30s and had over five years of work experience. I knew I wanted to take what I had learned over my career and apply it to a job in consulting, but I had to figure out what did I want to get out of the job. For me, I wanted to find a place where I could apply the leadership and experience I had right away, where I could continue to learn and grow from my colleagues and clients, and where I could do all of these things and also find ways to give back and contribute. A second-year at Georgetown urged me to apply for a coffee chat with Kearney, and as I started to research the firm and meet the people, I knew I had found the place for me – the summer internship experience just cemented what I had thought I would find out. Kearney is a top-tier firm that is a fraction of the size of its competitors – it has a strong entrepreneurial spirit and not a lot of red tape to get things done, and it has a culture of camaraderie and collaboration that felt welcoming to a 30-something-year-old new joiner. The culture and community of Kearney is also global – on any

given day, I'm speaking with folks in Australia, Colombia, France, Singapore, India, etc. You immediately understand that people want to help you so that we can all be successful together. Part of this is knowing that priorities change, and I just saw a lot of flexibility in the firm to have your career grow and change as your life does – whether it is family priorities, location, areas of interest, etc.

****

These are just some of the many factors to take into account when choosing a firm. Consider what is important to you and what aligns with your strengths. Build connections and have authentic conversations around these topics with consultants at your target firms. This will help you gain more clarity about the company and what decisions and priorities that consultant made. Prioritize these factors when considering a firm, but recognize that at different stages of your life, their weights may change.

7

SHOULD YOU CONSIDER A LARGE FIRM, MIDSIZED FIRM, OR BOUTIQUE FIRM?

Big fish in a small pond or small fish in a big pond? The size of the pond and the number of fish matter! Yet again, this is another "it depends" question where you need to bucket a number of factors, prioritize, and ultimately determine which firm is right for you and what trade-offs you are willing to make.

Let's begin by defining, in a very general sense, what you get with each of these options.

LARGE FIRM: SMALL FISH IN THE VAST OCEAN

A small fish can grow really large in the ocean, provided they avoid predators, don't lose focus and get lured away by distracting bait, and join a mutually supportive school of fish. Many are tempted to seek opportunities only at large firms – drawn by their brand and reputation; revenue and client opportunities; thought leadership, network, and training availability; and abundant salary and benefits that come with working for a "master of the universe" firm.

Large firms offer a wealth of expertise, an array of diversified services and skills, and countless learning and career pathways. Consultants who cut their teeth at a large firm gain credibility that can open doors for them in consulting and beyond, develop and strengthen skills and expertise that can help them advance, and have access to an expansive network. Those who advance in large firms will see their schools of support and influence grow, can gain outsized status in the firm and industry, and can pick from a host of opportunities. They will also likely see higher salaries, bonuses, and total compensation brought in by the hefty fees that these firms charge for their expertise.

But small fish have a lot of ocean to navigate. They need to build partnerships, find their place in the vast ocean, and determine where and how they get their sustenance. There is a lot of opportunity – and a lot of competition for that opportunity. Large firms have a huge talent pool, all looking to build their careers and advance in the consulting food chain. There are office politics, bureaucracy, and many paths to take. On the positive side, there are also countless resources to help you get there.

In general, at a large firm you should plan to get higher compensation, access to more training opportunities and resources, and a range of projects to help you build your experience. You should also expect to work longer hours (particularly when you factor in "corporate contributions"), may have a longer promotion timeline, and will likely be held to more structured metrics. As you advance, expect your responsibilities to increase, the pressure to increase, and the potential for burnout to also increase. The firm may also employ an up-or-out system where, if certain metrics are not met, you do not advance or are ultimately counseled out of the firm. Some people thrive in this environment and are able to build a roadmap to very long and successful careers there, many others plateau or burn out along the way and leave the firm or industry. Consider what you are looking to get out of the early stages of your career and then reassess as you advance.

BOUTIQUE/NICHE FIRM: BIG FISH, SMALL POND

While boutique firms may lack the brand, network, reach, and perhaps structured training opportunities of a large firm, they do offer specialization, deep functional or industry expertise, agility in meeting client demands, and a less hierarchical (pyramid) structure. At a smaller firm, you will be more likely to be put front and center with the client and will likely receive greater on-the-job training and direct client experience as a result of smaller, more focused projects. Your teams and firm may be more close-knit, as you know more of the fish in the pond. Your salary and total compensation may not be on par with those offered by large firms, but you may find that there are fewer expectations for "corporate contributions" and less competition in general to advance, which translates into better work-life balance. There may be more of an opportunity to get involved or lead efforts such as marketing, recruiting, business development, or internal professional development and thought leadership efforts. Generally, the organization may be flatter, which grants greater access to leaders, the freedom to initiate ideas, and the ability to gain deeper experience and focused expertise.

MIDSIZED FIRM: THE GREAT LAKE?

Staying with our bodies of water metaphor, medium firms can be more of a great lake – less breadth and depth of the ocean, but still a great deal of opportunity, expertise, and resources. These are often firms that have started small and have begun expanding aggressively through successful client accounts, growing their core markets and business lines and/or mergers and acquisitions. These firms may operate as hybrids and have certain characteristics beyond size that they use to differentiate themselves from both large and small firms. For example, medium sized firms may specialize in certain industry sectors or lines of business, they may offer some in-house training coupled with support for earning certifications outside of the firm, and the reach and reputation of their brand may be dependent on the industry or businesses they serve.

****

I'd recommend comparing the factors discussed above across the three categories to help you target firms. To recap:

- **Brand:** How does the firm market itself? What is the firm's reputation? What is its place in the market?
- **Culture:** Is the firm collaborative or competitive? Is there an up-or-out system?
- **Learning/Training:** How important is learning and growth to you? What opportunities does the firm provide for training, certifications, and professional development?
- **Network:** What's the firm's retention rate? Where do people go once they leave? What opportunities exist for people to network both within the company and beyond the company? What is the perception by outsiders of people who work at this firm? Does the firm have a structured way of keeping in touch with people who have left the firm (i.e., alumni network)?
- **Salary/Compensation/Benefits:** What is the salary relative to other companies? What is the bonus structure? What benefits exist? When the firm says "unlimited vacation time" is this really a way of enforcing billable targets and not compensating you for vacation that you are unable to use?
- **Trajectory:** What is the career track? How long does it typically take to get promoted? What factors does the firm consider when making

promotions? Is the firm a partnership model? What opportunities exist to advance and network within the firm?

- **Work-Life Balance:** Does the firm expect your work to intrude into your personal life? Do they expect you to work nights and weekends to get the job done? Are people taking calls and responding to email while "on vacation?" Does the firm actively help manage burnout, or are people encouraged to push through with performance structures that incentivize it?

MY OWN PATH

I look at this book as a letter to my younger self and as an opportunity to make amends for past mistakes, as well as help others invest in themselves and find the opportunities that set them up for a successful career. I did not always follow the advice I'm offering here, and some of these insights are based on hard lessons learned, heartache, and not optimizing my time. Many of these lessons also come through conversations, regrets, and lessons learned from colleagues in the industry. When I was looking at firms, I cast a wide net (keeping the metaphor going). I looked at all sorts of firms and did not necessarily evaluate by size and across all of these factors. Ultimately, I felt that I would adapt to any firm that I joined.

I ultimately joined a Big Five accounting firm that was building its management consulting practice. I liken this to a large firm incubating a startup or small practice that was focused on a particular industry. This particular situation helped illuminate the benefits and drawbacks of various sizes of firms. While I think I would have thrived in a pure large consulting firm, I also think there would have been sacrifices. I feel my competitive nature would have driven me to put in longer hours, set and push the pace, and learn and grow faster. It could have ended in burnout and diminishing work-life balance; it could have been an ongoing and unyielding pursuit to become partner; it could have been frustration at not breaking through the senior manager plateau and evaluating the critical decisions of whether or not to stick it out, join another firm, or take my consulting skills to another industry.

When I look back, I think I made the right decision at the time. Joining a small practice housed within a large firm enabled me to build a team, gain on-the-job training, develop and lead initiatives, and build relationships across the practice and firm. I supplemented the lack of structured training by obtaining professional certifications; contributed my own thought leadership to the practice and industry; and built my network by attending industry events, delivering workshops, and joining nonprofit boards to get more involved in my community. At a large firm, I think I would have pursued all of these experiences within the firm rather than externally. And I doubt *Case In Point: Government and Nonprofit* or this book would have been written because I would have been fixated on the firm and may have needed to go through rounds of approval for both books.

When I posed the question on what to look for when joining a firm and the pros and cons of firm size to Shelley Rappaport, my PBA colleague who had worked across the gamut of firms — from boutique, to large firm, to consulting think tank, to independent consultant, to entrepreneurial firm – she offered great advice on her seemingly circuitous route:

> There are pros and cons to weigh for each, and you really need to focus on where you can be successful. The larger firms have a brand, infrastructure, and resources and that may be what you need to grow and develop. A smaller firm may have more opportunity to get involved, and this could lead to a faster career trajectory. When I joined or left firms, the most important factor to me was culture. I wanted to know that the leaders of the firm were creating a culture and had a personal value system that aligned with my own. As I grew in my career, I could be more selective and choose a firm that was open, transparent, and collaborative. They listen and course correct, and that is something that I value more than the brand or title.

****

Consultants are adaptable and can craft their place in whatever ecosystem they are a part of, and when that ecosystem is no longer meeting their needs, they can adapt again or change their environment. Selecting the environment that you are starting in is a critical part of crafting your career.

8

ARE YOU A BETTER FIT FOR PRIVATE-SECTOR, PUBLIC-SECTOR, OR NONPROFIT CONSULTING?

After six months of trying to connect with a friend who had just launched her career with one of the coveted MBB consulting firms (McKinsey, Bain, Boston Consulting Group), we finally found time for her to come over on a Sunday to catch up and watch football. I was eager to hear how her project was going and what her experience was like landing her dream job at one of these exclusive firms. She was impeccably credentialed, brilliant, personable, and with an unparalleled work ethic. She had to have been crushing it!

She came by nearly an hour later than expected and brought a friend – her laptop. As she crunched numbers and set up pivot tables and produced slides with football on in the background, I tried to ask her how things were going. She had been on the road for most of this project, coming back on weekends to try to have a semblance of a life in Washington, DC. As we were catching up between slides, her phone buzzed. She answered and started talking through her slides and line of thinking before ending with, "I'll make those changes and turn it around in the next 20 minutes." As she started furiously typing away, her phone buzzed again and she got up and stepped outside to talk through the slides some more. When she came back five minutes later, she began typing even more furiously, making up for those five minutes of lost productivity.

I watched out of the corner of my eye (football was on) – awed, dismayed, and a bit perplexed. Most aspiring consultants would consider her position to be their dream job. People fought tooth and nail to land a berth at her firm, to rise to the top of the consulting food chain, and stamp this impressive brand on their resume. And here was my brilliant friend, working 90 hours a week and trying to find time to catch up with a friend between the mountain of tasks she had to complete on the weekend. Her productivity-maximizing brain thought that bringing her laptop and cell phone, and getting some work done while catching up, would be a good idea. I think both of us left that catch-up session more stressed.

This set me thinking about whether a private-sector firm was for me. While my friend may have dimmed my view of it, generally speaking, private-sector consulting did have some advantages. There is at least a perception that a job in the private sector was more prestigious – it's selective, higher-paying, and you got the added "bonus" that comes with being on the road four days or so a week for project work. Private-sector consultants are the "masters of the universe" whose recommendations fuel product decisions, profits, and losses. B-school students vie for these positions – spending hours networking, preparing for case interviews, and learning about the firm. And there are other pluses: (1) the compensation and bonus structure seemed to be higher, (2) these are selective jobs where the firms often invest significantly in your training, (3) more doors are opened to transfer into other industries or move in-house for companies, (4) firms offer travel and the savings that come with the per diem lifestyle, and (5) you get to form a network of people who were going to run the business world.

On the flip slide, this culture could translate into long hours on the road and perfecting presentations with profit as a primary motive. If these and the example of my friend above are not a good fit for you, public-sector and/or nonprofit sector consulting may be options.

While there tend to be shorter hours, less travel, and less round-the-clock expectations in the public sector, the project engagements serve as another major distinction. Private-sector projects tend to be rapid, three- to six-month efforts that quickly boost productivity, lead to a product launch, or build strategy. These shorter-term, fast-paced engagements are usually less hampered by bureaucracy and enable consultants to get an array of project experience. Conversely, public-sector contracts tend to last longer – typically one year with up to four option years. This enables a public-sector consultant to build stronger relationships with a client over the longer-term engagement, contribute to different aspects of the client or project team, and stay from the beginning to the end of a project. Less attractive: Public-sector engagements can be bureaucratic and consensus-driven, which means the pace may be slower and consultants need to negotiate byzantine politics to get their recommendations across. Consulting in the public sector, you run the risk of getting pigeonholed with a particular project, client, or industry, building depth of experience, but not necessarily breadth of experience.

Public-sector and nonprofit consulting are distinct in that you are often working for mission-driven organizations that are looking to maximize their impact or do more with their budget (while this is not to say that private-sector companies cannot have a mission, there is often a profit incentive that is associated with these projects). The compensation and bonus structure are typically not as generous, but when you do the math, you may actually come out ahead on an hourly rate. The hours are typically not as long, since many people in the government and nonprofit industries stick to a more regular nine-to-five schedule (and this is not to say that these individuals are not working extremely hard at their jobs). Many of the projects are based in Washington, DC, or nonprofit epicenters, which means that if you live near one of these areas, your travel is limited.

There are also differences in the opportunities that public-sector consulting unlocks. My observation of the industry has led me to the conclusion that private sector may offer more paths than public-sector and nonprofit, and many public-sector and nonprofit clients and organizations seek to operate more "like the private sector" because the scope of projects and experience is broader. I've also noted an unfair stigma often attached to public-sector and nonprofit consulting as do-gooders who bring a less-valued mentality. All of this translates into being easier to transition from private sector to public-sector and nonprofit than the reverse. At the same time, public-sector and nonprofit consulting opens a different set of doors – many leave the industry for active roles in government and nonprofit.

✳✳✳✳✳✳✳✳

When I was evaluating whether to apply to private- or public-sector consulting firms, I was attracted by the fast-paced world of the private sector. The prestige, travel, and types of projects appealed to me. However, when I evaluated what was most important to me, public-sector and nonprofit work seemed to be the better fit. From a client standpoint, I was far more interested in social good and helping an organization better meet its mission of helping people rather than helping a company sell more dog food. From a work-life balance standpoint, I was ready to start setting roots and building a footprint in a community and saw Washington, DC, as a viable home. I had built a network and lasting friendships here, and the more regular hours and less frequent travel obligations would give me time to hustle and have fun with friends. I saw community as extending beyond life in the organization and wanted to build community both within and outside of my firm. While money was important, particularly since I had graduated from business school with nearly $200,000 in loans, I did the math and was comfortable with a longer payback period for what I anticipated would be greater work-life balance. So while I knew public-sector and nonprofit consulting might cause me to be pigeonholed and could pose added challenges should I ever want to transition into the private sector, I was comfortable with that career choice. (And I was right about being pigeonholed. When I considered private-sector consulting, several consulting firms and private-sector roles would turn me down because I lacked private-sector consulting experience. Yet that probably ended up being a blessing for me.)

****

In the end, selecting whether to be in the private sector or public sector depends on your unique priorities. I've seen very talented people get burned out by the relentless pace of private-sector consulting as well as by the bureaucracy of the public sector and nonprofit industry. Both are viable career options, and I'd recommend exploring both to determine which will fit you best. Do your research, set up coffee chats, and evaluate which factors are most important to you.

9
WHICH BUSINESS LINE SHOULD YOU CONSIDER?

L et's start with the old consulting answer – it depends. Most firms, particularly the larger ones, are broken down by industry and by solution offerings. These solutions or service lines often are some variation of (1) strategy and operations, (2) human capital, and (3) technology. Nearly every project you work on will have some sort of strategy or process element, a people side, and a technology component. When considering which business line is right for you, start by asking yourself how you approach a problem. Do you see a problem as fundamentally a function of the processes behind that problem? Do you find that if people are effective, the problem is resolved? Do you feel that technology provides the right solution?

STRATEGY AND OPERATIONS (S&O): PROCESS DRIVES RESULTS

Strategy and operations projects tend to be very analytical and focus on developing the right strategy, objectives, and supporting actions to achieve a desired result. They're about optimizing processes or building a plan that incrementally moves an organization toward its goals. Consultants in this business line tend to be very methodical and metric-driven. They are analytical and look for quantitative and qualitative data to evaluate the current state of the effort and to help shape the future state of the organization. Common S&O projects may include working on a 3–5 year strategic plan that prioritizes actions and resources, reviewing a process and identifying areas of waste or ways the process could be reengineered to operate more efficiently, reviewing market share, and evaluating prospective mergers and acquisitions or market growth strategies to increase market share.

HUMAN CAPITAL: IT'S ALL ABOUT THE PEOPLE

Human capital consultants look at projects through a people-centered lens. Their projects focus much more on the behavioral and qualitative side of the business and tend to center on how to attract, select, recruit, train, and promote people, as well as incentivize them to perform. There is a lot of psychology, empathy, and communication associated with these projects. While all consultants need to exhibit strong interpersonal skills and emotional intelligence, perhaps it is most important in this business line. Human capital consultants are often dealing very closely with people who are undergoing a change, so they need to be adept at projecting confidence, proactively addressing uncertainty, and building coalitions to guide change. Common human capital projects may include determining the core knowledge and skills that an organization needs to prepare for the workforce of the future, aligning incentives and performance metrics to increase employee output, designing training, and crafting communications that help an organization prepare for a major organizational change.

TECHNOLOGY: IMPLEMENTING THE FUTURE

Technology projects focus on building the right IT solutions and associated behaviors to address a complex business challenge. Technology consultants tend to be agile with an eye toward human-centered design, the ability to capture requirements to make a system function, and skills to iterate and adapt solutions to the customer's needs. Their projects are often under tight timelines, and they often have to battle with scope that can quickly creep beyond project expectations. Technology consultants need to have strong technical skills and understanding, while also be able to balance risk and project management. Common technology consulting projects include designing and implementing a CRM system to track data and key touchpoints for the client, building a technology platform that helps document and track approvals and orders for a product, or developing a donor database to track relationships and actions in regard to current and prospective donors and prospective grants for a nonprofit.

****

I've worked in and across all these business lines at various stages of my career. While I find myself gravitating more toward the people side of business challenges, the skills and understanding needed for all these lines are complementary and mutually reinforcing. When you consider a business challenge, or even a challenge in your daily life, how do you approach it? Do you look for the latest app to help you change your behavior? Do you try to develop a habit or process? Do you think through incentives and how to best motivate yourself? When you read about business challenges in the news, which solution comes to mind? How would you have approached that problem? Consider these situations and find people in the industry to talk with and learn more about the types of projects they work on, problems they solve, and why they chose their particular business line.

10

HOW DO YOU SELECT AN OFFICE LOCATION?

Many firms, particularly the larger ones, have multiple office locations. Where you want to work is yet another decision to make in crafting your career, and your career trajectory could depend in part on the office you select. When considering a possible location, it is important to consider: (1) office size and growth trajectory, (2) office relationships, (3) industry alignment, and, perhaps most importantly, (4) personal preference. While the first three may be more closely tied to your career and place in the firm, ultimately, you may more heavily weight your preference based on proximity to family, friends, or affinity for that particular location.

OFFICE SIZE AND GROWTH TRAJECTORY

Considering office size and growth trajectory often brings up the big fish in a small pond, or small fish in a large pond conundrum. A smaller office may offer more opportunities for connections and building stronger relationships, while a larger office may enable you to build a more expansive network and open more avenues for projects, business lines, or industries. One important consideration is to view how quickly the office is growing. Office performance can often be a factor in salary and bonuses and could play a role in promotions. For instance, if an office is performing above forecasts, people in that office may see higher salary increases or bonuses. The office could also get greater visibility or grow, which could lead to people being promoted at a faster rate to support that growth. If an office is slated for growth, you may be able to get in on the ground level and help build out an office and team, quickly establishing yourself as a respected veteran in that office.

OFFICE RELATIONSHIPS

When thinking about your personal board of advisors, one thing to consider is who could be an advisor within your own company. Is there someone higher up who referred you for the position? Is there a connection that you made? Did you connect well with someone who interviewed and ultimately hired you? These are people who might have a vested interest in your success and could potentially become members of your PBA. Consider which office they're based in and if they would be willing to help you navigate your career in that office and beyond. Also, consider external relationships that you may have in that city and whether or not you could build these relationships if you lived and worked there. Some offices may also be led by a visible and respected leader in the firm. Being a part of this office may have a halo effect as their star power rubs off on you, or you could find yourself with a valuable mentor to help you grow your career. Consider the leaders of each office and how they are contributing to their clients, developing thought leadership, building their teams, and supporting their teams. To re-emphasize Shelley Rappaport's words, culture is extremely important, and offices may take on the culture of their leaders for better or for worse.

INDUSTRY OR BUSINESS ALIGNMENT

If you want to pursue a particular practice, business line, or industry, consider the location of offices aligned with that career goal (for instance, if you know you want to do public sector consulting, Washington DC, may make the most sense; if you are targeting energy, then you may look into Texas; choosing technology might bring you to San Francisco). Many consulting firms have people geographically dispersed and have hubs for particular practices or industries. There may also be clients with headquarters clustered in a particular location (technology – Silicon Valley, healthcare – Cleveland, higher education – Boston, financial services – New York, etc.) where you may want to work with limited travel. Moving to these areas could give you the opportunity to build your network and specialize in a particular industry.

PERSONAL PREFERENCE

At the end of the day, the most important factor for you may be where you ultimately want to live. This could be driven by proximity to family, closeness to friends, costs of living, your favorite sports team, etc. You may decide the Chicago winters are just not for you even though the area is a great match on other factors. When I was advising a recent consultant hire on office location, it seemed like the stars aligned on one particular office. He had built a relationship with a partner in this office, the industry he was most interested in had an established practice there, and it was slated for growth. Yet while he may have had better possibilities for advancing in the "stars aligned" office, he ultimately decided that he would be happier living in a different city where several of his closest friends lived. Two years later, he is doing well and was recently promoted. His industry and the types of projects that he works on have shifted a bit from his original preference, but in consulting you do not always get to choose your clients.

Yashomati Bachul Koul, a principal in Kearney's San Francisco office, made a similar decision. Koul interned in New York, and while they loved the city and had family on the East Coast, Koul and their wife ultimately decided on San Francisco. When I asked what drove this decision, they shared,

> There are always those whispers that you should start in a particular office because you could have "better" access to leadership or a higher likelihood of staying utilized/staffed. I did my internship in New York and was feeling conflicted on whether or not to stay in New York and continue to build my network. I had the blessing of having a mentor who said, "This job is incredibly demanding; live where you want to go home." When I was traveling, the feeling that I got to return to a place that I loved was what did it for me. My wife loves it here, we have great weather, fantastic friends. It's the old concept of the virtuous cycle. Where does this start? For me, it starts with when I am a happier human being. I am providing better client service, which leads to longer-lasting relationships, which leads to greater career success. A lot of people overthink everything. Consultants overthink everything and sometimes it is very simple: Live where you want to go home.

****

As with any decision, you have to balance the trade-offs and consider how you prioritize each factor. Some things that you prioritize now, may not be the same that you prioritize 3–5 years from now. Having insight into the operations and structure of the firms and offices can help you make a better-informed decision that can pay dividends in the projects you support, the people you meet, the networks you build, and the salary, bonuses, and other benefits that you receive.

11

SHOULD YOU CONSIDER AN OFFICE ABROAD?

One approach that I have seen classmates, colleagues, and mentees have success with is applying to an overseas office. This can be particularly effective for the highly selective MBB firms (McKinsey, Bain, Boston Consulting Group), where it can be an opportunity to get a foot in the door. If you are at a core school (a school where the firm recruits heavily), then this strategy could increase your chances of getting an offer. If you are not at a core school, this could make you stand out and increase your chances of getting an interview. Firms that hire you for a particular office, invest time and training in you, and have seen you perform over a period of time may ultimately try to retain you if you seek to align with a different office. You may also find that you have built solid relationships and enjoy working and living abroad. Finally, you may ultimately determine that after a few years working for the firm abroad, you can cash in on the brand and training received and apply internally for another office or be marketable externally for another firm or company. When considering an office abroad, you should review (1) selectivity, (2) experience alignment, and (3) your long-term plan.

SELECTIVITY: DOES AN OFFICE ABROAD POSITION YOU FOR AN OFFER?

Whether an overseas assignment will better position you for an offer is a question that can often be answered in a coffee chat with a recruiter or connection at the firm. Certain offices have a high demand for US-educated aspiring consultants – and limited supply as these consultants seek alignment to New York, Chicago, San Francisco, and other US offices. Learn if there are particular offices that are seeking US-educated consultants and see if you can help them to meet the supply-demand gap.

In a real-world example, one consultant started his career by applying for an internship in Russia for Bain. He knew his experience and education would be in high demand there. He received the internship offer and spent the summer in Moscow performing at a high level, building relationships, and gaining from the brand and experience of a highly coveted firm. He returned to the United States with experience and training from a prestigious firm and was instantly more marketable for full-time hiring at other top consulting firms. The summer internship proved that he could succeed abroad, but also had the added effect of raising his stock for positions in the US for Bain and top-tier competitors.

EXPERIENCE ALIGNMENT: DO YOU KNOW HOW TO CONDUCT BUSINESS IN THIS COUNTRY?

Once you have identified overseas offices where there is high demand, determine if you have the experience and qualifications to work in them. Are there language requirements? Are they seeking certain experience and expertise? Is citizenship required? If you have dual citizenship, speak the language, and/or have worked with companies and on projects conducting business in this region (or studied abroad in this country or region), you can position yourself well for one of these consulting roles. Consider whether the office focuses on an industry or business line that you would like to work in and if you understand or are aligned closely with the culture or business values of that location. Also, if you are planning to transfer to the United States, see where that business line may correspond with offices in the States and make sure that there is an office you'd want to seek an internal transfer to.

Back to our consultant: After he had succeeded in his internship overseas, he tried to parlay that experience into a full-time offer in the US. He found that although his experience in Moscow directly correlated to the Houston office, Houston was a less-than-ideal location for him. He applied to the three prestigious MBB firms with a heavy preference on getting an offer in Boston, New York, or Washington, DC. Reflecting on his possible choices, he felt his skills best aligned with McKinsey, his network best aligned with Boston Consulting Group, and his experience best aligned with his overseas internship at Bain. The only offer he received for a full-time position was another overseas posting. When he evaluated this against offers from other firms in the US, he decided that the internship had already enabled him to test-drive working overseas and that an offer from a top-tier firm would provide the brand, network, and training to prepare him for longer-term success in consulting. He accepted the full-time offer for the overseas role and never looked back!

LONG-TERM PLAN: WHAT IS YOUR STRATEGY IF YOU RECEIVE AN OFFER?

You've identified an office abroad that is seeking someone of your caliber, credentials, and background. You understand the culture and office and believe you can be successful serving as a consultant in this office. And you've considered the financial practicalities (for example, part of your long-term plan should be understanding compensation differentials – some firms may entice you with benefits such as housing or you have a larger real take-home pay due to tax differences). The stars align, and you receive an offer – now what?

Even though you accepted an overseas position in the hopes that you would be taken into the firm, don't try to alchemize this offer into an internal transfer to another office right off the bat. Pulling this bait-and-switch move could leave a bad taste and could damage your long-term relationship with the company. Expect that you are likely committing at least a year (and in some cases, longer) to the office abroad. During that year, you should build relationships, learn and grow, and receive stellar performance reviews. This will strengthen your bargaining power if you are looking to transfer to another office. A firm does not want to lose someone in whom it has invested time and training and who is showing leadership potential. The firm will be more willing to offer an office relocation if you start actively building a plan after you have proven yourself. Another option may be to leverage the brand and training that you have received to go to another firm or serve as an in-house consultant for a company in your desired location. You should join this office location with an open mind and may ultimately enjoy the relationships you have built, life abroad, and opportunities from this office.

Let's see how this strategy worked for our consultant. He had performed admirably overseas for nearly two years. He saw how several consultants had started in the overseas office but soon after requested an internal transfer to US offices. Not only was this frowned upon, but also hampered their relationships with the firm. Observing this, and using his emotional intelligence skills, this consultant bided his time. He received strong performance reviews, built solid relationships, and after putting in valuable sweat equity, he raised the idea of transfer. He not only built a business case after the firm was already invested in him, but also made sure to time it when that office was looking to move some of their consultants. After nearly two years overseas, he would move to the ultra-competitive New York City office for one of the most respected firms. Less than five years later, he would be a partner at another reputable firm.

****

An office abroad may be a viable option for getting your foot in the door, particularly if the firm is very selective and you meet the requirements. You should develop a long-term plan of how this office will help you advance, whether as a long-term consultant at that office, a consultant transferring to a different office, or as someone who moves up the ladder and leverages their experience for a different company down the road. Go in with an open mind and evaluate these options as you prove your value to the office and firm. Make sure you have built relationships, excelled, and put in sweat equity before raising the option of an internal transfer!

12

HOW DO YOU RESPOND TO REJECTION?

Rejection is part of life for aspiring consultants. Your target firm does not offer you an internship or full-time offer. Your client does not take your recommendations. You don't get staffed on the project you were vying for. You get counseled out of a firm. Consultants develop a thick skin, capture feedback, and use this feedback to become better teammates and better versions of themselves. They also have to adapt quickly to the situation and perform the alchemy of turning challenges into opportunities. Approach rejection as feedback and a chance to learn and grow. Each rejection unlocks another opportunity.

I've experienced rejection throughout my career. It's disappointing, but more disappointing than rejection is not gaining a lesson from it. When firms that I had built strong relationships with did not extend an offer, I looked inward and broke down the situation. Did I not present myself in the best possible way? How did I respond to questions – were my answers open to interpretation, and could I have answered in a different way? Did I come on too strong, or not strong enough? Trying to step outside your own ego and view the situation from someone else's perspective can help you gain a valuable lesson that makes you better.

For instance, I remember that in one interview (where I did receive an offer), as I was waiting to be introduced to the interviewer, the executive assistant made a gesture to fix my tie (it was a humid DC day and I had loosened it a bit). This little piece of feedback reminded me to find a mirror and give myself a once-over before stepping into an interview. During another interview, in an effort to build a connection with the interviewer, I probably overshared on a story. This experience helped me to better read the room and craft stories that are memorable and authentic – but not too personal. After another interview, I had the opportunity to take the elevator down with the interviewer. She had dug in on one of my responses, and I realized that the way I worded it might have been perceived as a red flag or lack of interest in the firm. While I provided more context during that elevator ride, I was not surprised that I didn't get the offer. Interviews are difficult because the interviewer has limited context and will craft a narrative based on your responses. Tell stories that leave them with the narrative that shows your best.

There are countless times when I have delivered (what I thought were) foolproof recommendations to a client, only to have these recommendations rejected. While it was disappointing to spend months on a project and provide thorough recommendations that were ultimately dismissed, it allowed me to sharpen my craft. I've devoted more time to testing recommendations up front with clients, gaining buy-in and feedback, and even leaving breadcrumbs to help the client reach the conclusion on their own. I've varied communications strategies – using stories, raising risks, benchmarking, highlighting quantitative analysis, utilizing a coalition – to help drive recommendations.

****

Andrew Synnott has had a very successful consulting career and has been an outstanding leader and mentor. His leadership has inspired and driven a number of consultants. I personally learned a great deal about consulting from him when he served as president of the Consulting Club at Georgetown's McDonough School of Business. Andrew helped aspiring consultants build plans to land the roles they wanted, provided feedback to strengthen their skills, and built connections that opened doors for the Georgetown network. He is one of the most brilliant and articulate people I have ever come across. Yet he was once counseled out of a top-tier firm after less than two years in the role, although he had worked exceedingly hard to land this job and worked perhaps even harder once he earned it. Yet because he looked at rejection as way to learn, his disappointment ushered in a new beginning. While Andrew certainly had the credentials to land another top-tier consulting offer, he made the conscious decision to seek roles in industry. Reflecting on why the match with the consulting firm was not right, he took valuable lessons around researching the offices, teams, and building relationships prior to making this important career decision. Andrew carried the growth, learning, and contacts made in consulting to his new in-house strategy and operations role for a major company. He was able to purpose the brand, network, resources, and experiences earned through the consulting gauntlet to a role that he ultimately felt better suited for. Rejection was only a temporary roadblock for him, and this short-term obstacle opened a path to longer-term prosperity, greater work-life balance, happiness, and success. Andrew advises people who face this type of rejection to not view it as the end of the world, but just the start of another journey.

****

When you face rejection, reframe it as an opportunity to learn and grow. Look inward and review the rejection from the perspective of other stakeholders (interviewer, client, project manager). Get feedback from a peer or colleague and see if you are reading the situation in the same way or able to gain a distinct perspective. Allow yourself to be vulnerable. To paraphrase vulnerability expert Brené Brown, vulnerability is the opposite of weakness; it is recalling times of great courage. Allowing yourself to be vulnerable – to be courageous in recalling times of fear, uncertainty, or rejection – will enable you to advance in your career and grow as a leader.

13

HOW DO YOU DEVELOP A 3-5 YEAR PLAN?

Businesses, nonprofit organizations, and higher education institutions all have strategic plans to prioritize scarce time and resources, hold themselves accountable, and progress for the future. Individuals can follow this example by developing their own 3–5 year strategic plan that they regularly review, adapt to changing situations, and evaluate against their timeline. Generally, you can develop a career strategic plan by looking at your current state, determining your vision for the future, developing a gap analysis, and action planning to address those gaps.

CURRENT STATE: WHERE AM I NOW?

Start with a thorough assessment of where you are now:

- What are your strengths?
- What are your areas of improvement?
- What do you enjoy doing? How do you spend your leisure time?
- How are you spending your time now?
- What career prospects do you have?
- How are you advancing in your career (promotion, learning, financially)?
- What obstacles are you currently facing (time, money, knowledge, skills, network, credentials)?

Taking a holistic approach of where you are now will help you establish your foundation and starting point. Once you know where you are, you can better plan for where you are going.

FUTURE STATE: WHERE DO I WANT TO BE 3-5 YEARS FROM NOW?

Consider your idealized vision for the future. Do you intend to switch careers? Do you want to advance in your current career? Do you want to develop a side hustle? Allow that future to begin to crystallize in your mind. Develop a clear vision statement of what you would like to accomplish in the next 3–5 years.

- Do you want to have a specific title?
- Do you want to have credentials or established expertise?
- Do you have a target salary?
- Do you want greater work-life balance?

As you craft your idealized vision for the future, recognize that there will be constraints and you may need to make trade-off decisions. As I've already noted, time is our scarcest commodity and most valuable resource, and you may not be able to devote all the time needed for you to accomplish this vision in this time period (and that's OK).

GAP ANALYSIS: HOW FAR IS "WHERE I AM" FROM "WHERE I WANT TO BE"?

Once you've done these two evaluations, you'll immediately start to notice some distinctions between where you are and where you want to be. Perhaps there is a huge gap in knowledge or skills. Maybe you recognize that there is a significant time commitment to developing the right credentials. While the gap may seem like a vast abyss, part of the fun is problem-solving (are you seeing a theme?). Just like a consultant, you can consult for yourself and develop a plan to help you address these gaps.

ACTION PLANNING: HOW DO I GET TO WHERE I WANT TO BE?

This is often the most challenging part of crafting your plan and, when developed, something that you should review regularly to ensure that you are still on track. Start by breaking down your vision into three to five critical objectives. For each objective, prioritize three to five actions to that will help you to achieve that objective. When developing these actions, make sure that they are SMART:

- **Specific:** They are clear and have established boundaries.
- **Measurable:** They have a defined output (work product, completion, time, volume, quantity, etc.).
- **Actionable:** There are steps that you can take to complete these actions and help you get closer to your objective.
- **Relevant:** They directly relate to the objective and are aligned with your goal.
- **Timely:** There is a specific time frame for achieving this action.

Regularly reviewing these objectives and actions builds in accountability. It helps you to ensure that your objectives and actions are still relevant and to evaluate whether or not you need to pivot. It also ensures that you are tracking your progress and adjusting course. Because time is your most precious resource, you need to prioritize and dedicate time to the areas that are going to help you move toward your goals. What you need to focus on may not always be the area of greatest impact (at least not immediately), as there may be some dependencies and critical steps that you need to take initially that will pay dividends and better prepare you for higher impact actions in the future.

****

I developed my first 3–5 year plan after graduating from college. I established a vision where I would have a master's degree and leverage my strengths in a career that would enable me to contribute to a mission-oriented organization. Admittedly, this vision was a bit vague, and as a wide-eyed recent graduate ready to tackle the world, I was unsure of which path my career would take. I knew that I needed to gain some work experience to better understand the avenues available and I also knew that I wanted to continue to learn, grow, and earn education credentials that would help me take that next step in my career. With that vision in mind, I began to develop objectives that would help me to better qualify and achieve that vision.

First, I developed an objective around social impact. I wanted a role where I felt that I could contribute to a community, take ownership, and help others. Finance was one of the "hot" jobs in 2007, on the precipice of the Great Recession, and while I initially considered roles in finance, I crossed several companies off my list because they did not help me meet this objective.

Second, I created an objective around learning and growth. I wanted a role that would challenge me, help me develop leadership skills, open opportunities to contribute, and enable me to evaluate master's programs. I had considered a law degree and was also considering an MBA, and I wanted to take time to evaluate those programs (and others) before making a significant financial and time investment.

Third, I formed an objective around building my network, identifying mentors, advocates, and people who could help me evaluate master's programs, career avenues, and enhance performance in my current role.

Building this vision and establishing these objectives focused me on several career options. One seemed to meet each of these objectives – Teach For America. For those unfamiliar with TFA, it's a program akin to the Peace Corps, where recent college graduates commit to teaching at least two years in an underresourced school. TFA's theory of change is that the nation's education achievement gap is so pervasive that it requires talented and creative leaders committed to learning, receiving training, and addressing this gap as teachers and taking their experience after those two years to continue to address the achievement gap as educators, entrepreneurs, policymakers, business leaders, and advocates. TFA highly emphasized perseverance, leadership, and growth. It is as selective as some of the nation's top colleges, has an expansive network, and provided an opportunity to earn a master's in education. Most importantly, it enabled me to directly impact a community. Although I had initially considered a career in finance or business, setting goals and objectives drove my decision. TFA seemed to meet all of my objectives and more, and many of its alumni were now leaders in education, business, nonprofit, and social entrepreneurship. Using my vision and objectives as a guide, I joined TFA in New York City and was able to start building a roadmap of supporting actions.

TFA certainly provided opportunities for social impact and enabled me to connect with like-minded, mission-driven leaders. As I reviewed this objective, I considered specific actions that I could take to get involved. While my first year would be inwardly focused on my school, community, and TFA, I began to look outward as I developed confidence and competency as a teacher. I volunteered for organizations like Minds Matter (providing mentoring and coaching to students from low-income communities), Prep For Prep (providing tutoring to high-performing underrepresented students placed in elite high schools), The Posse Foundation (being a part of its dynamic assessment process to determine which underrepresented students would receive a scholarship and join a "posse" of nine others to provide peer support), and got involved in recruiting, event planning, resource development, and fundraising for TFA. This enabled me to not only build a deeper understanding of how organizations were addressing the ubiquitous challenge of the achievement gap, but also allowed me to compare business models, theories of change, and impact strategies.

Volunteering and getting involved in social impact efforts created a flywheel of learning and growth and also helped me build my network. I addressed my learning and growth objective by earning my master's in the Science of Teaching as part of the TFA program. Additionally, commute time turned into prime reading time, and I became a vociferous reader of business and management books and began seeing how I could apply these principles to my classroom and daily life. As a teacher, learning is constant and you incorporate lessons learned into how you instruct. This became a key part of my growth, with students sometimes being my fiercest critics and best feedback channels on how I presented material. As I became more comfortable teaching, I began to look outward as well – attending workshops and sessions, being selected for the New Leaders Council (NLC) fellowship, and identifying further actions to support learning and growth.

My third objective centered around building my network and skills. TFA had built partnerships with a number of companies that offered summer internships to corps members interested in exploring other careers. I leveraged these partnerships by applying for a number of roles in finance. As I waited to hear back from my final-round interviews with Lehman Brothers and Morgan Stanley, the market collapsed. This was the spring of 2008, and I remember picking up a newspaper with the headline that Lehman Brothers would be laying off 15,000 people. I got a call later that day that I would not be receiving an offer. Finance had been one avenue I was interested in learning more about, and as that door closed, I got more involved in the business side of TFA, joining its summer training operations staff. My role focused on developing and improving processes, enhancing communications, and supporting a team of dedicated educators training aspiring teachers. This not only enabled me to improve my own craft, but also to begin to develop valuable business skills. I leveraged the TFA network to learn more about other business professions (including consulting), joined the advisory board of an education technology startup, and continued to pursue summer business roles with TFA. While I had to adapt my approach in the face of the Great Recession, TFA afforded me numerous avenues to build my network, advance my skills, and pursue opportunities to apply these skills. And despite the recession, New York was also constantly bustling with opportunity.

By the end of my third year of teaching, my actions surrounding my objectives began to crystallize around a plan. I enjoyed the business of social impact and solving complex challenges. Looking back to my initial vision, I felt that I had enough information and experiences to invest in an MBA and pursue a career in social-sector consulting. My fourth year of teaching would include applying to business schools. By the start of the fifth year of my initial plan, I would be entering Georgetown's McDonough School of Business as a full-time MBA candidate. This would formalize the closure of my first strategic

plan and the launch of my next 3–5 year plan, which would take me through my MBA and planning, launching, and crafting my consulting career.

LAUNCHING YOUR CONSULTING CAREER

YOUR FIRST 3-5 YEARS

My first 3–5 year plan took me from a newly minted college graduate through four years of teaching as a member of TFA. As I started my MBA at Georgetown's McDonough School of Business, I began thinking through my next five-year plan. At the end of them, I hoped to have completed my transformation from teacher to management consultant, be advancing toward a leadership role in a consulting firm, and be sharing insights and lessons learned with professionals and aspiring consultants. I began mapping out networks, MBA club activity and leadership roles that I could contribute to, and courses that would help me advance my skills. Many of the lessons learned in the previous section came from this formative time and the countless conversations that I've had with both aspiring consultants and those who had recently launched their consulting careers. Some of these were hard lessons learned from missteps and inexperience (lessons I wish had been shared with me as I launched my career). Others were lessons shared by more seasoned consultants that benefited me during these early years. Still others I learned from witnessing successful consultants forge ahead in their careers. As more and more aspiring and new consultants asked me for guidance, I thought it would be valuable to share feedback at scale and map out my own journey, some of the common decisions and crossroads that need to be considered, and how I evaluated decisions. My hope is that this section will build on the foundational "Planning Your Consulting Career" section, unlock insights, save you precious time, and position you for a successful career.

Whether you aspire to make partner, go independent or in-house, or advance until you decide to pivot, this section will provide you with a roadmap for navigating and crafting your career and will help you shape your next 3–5 year plan in consulting.

14

WHAT DO YOU CONSIDER WHEN NEGOTIATING?

Let's say you have an offer (and hopefully many!). Congratulations! Your first step toward launching your career starts now, before you accept any offer – and that's negotiation. With any offer comes the opportunity to negotiate. Recognize that a negotiation does not have to be high-pressure or combative and can pay huge dividends. For instance, an hour or so of benchmarking, doing your research to compare offers across organizations (or even between companies if you have received multiple offers), and sharing information with human resources can lead to a sizable increase in salary. That hour or so of preparation can net an extremely high ROI and perhaps hundreds of thousands of compounded dollars over the course of your career. Perhaps your negotiation nets you $5,000 extra a year in salary. First, that amount compounds over time, as each year you are getting that $5,000 on top of what the firm initially offered you. Second, if your salary increases by a percentage each year, you'll be getting a higher increase as a result of a higher initial salary. So negotiate!

Yet despite the obvious benefits, and while negotiating is becoming more commonplace, a *Harvard Business Review* report "Nice Girls Don't Ask"[2] found that only 57% of highly educated men and 7% of highly educated women negotiate! That's a lot of people leaving money on the table. There may be many reasons why people don't negotiate – they are grateful to receive the job offer, they don't feel that they have other options, they fear starting off on the wrong foot with the company, or they simply don't know what to do. Overcome these barriers by recognizing that negotiating may the highest ROI you can get for your time, that your starting salary can determine your financial trajectory, and that many companies leave some wiggle room in anticipation of you negotiating.

To negotiate successfully, you have to be prepared. Ensure that you (1) do your research, (2) have multiple levers to pull, and (3) approach the negotiation as a shared problem that you are trying to solve.

DO YOUR RESEARCH

Know your worth! Prer Bania is a director of Digital Strategy, host of the *Career by Design* podcast, and founder of Inspiration Careers (https://www. inspirationcareers.com/), a career coaching practice that provides the "tools and support to take things to the next level." She has faced and advised on many negotiations over the course of her career. Prer has been a coach and thought partner to me (remember your personal board of advisors!), and her experience has helped shape many of my career choices. When discussing negotiations, Prer notes, "Negotiations start by negotiating with yourself. Know your worth. Know your target and don't settle. Sell yourself on that value first so that you can be confident selling others on your worth!" Use resources like Glassdoor or people in your network to get a sense for what comparable salaries are at other companies for similar roles. Prer advises, "Be very intentional about the full package and recognize any benefit has a monetary value. Oftentimes, people forget this and end up getting a lower total package as a result." Don't forget to compare the full package!

- Do other companies tend to offer a signing bonus?
- What is the typical year-end bonus?
- What benefits does the company offer?
- How much vacation is typically offered?
- How many hours are you generally working a week?
- What is the cost of living in the office location and how does this compare to the salary?

You can use your understanding of a comparable company as a reference point and benchmark in your negotiation. Moreover, review and compare position descriptions and expectations for similar roles and use them as benchmarks. Try to find differentiators that place you on a higher footing than these benchmarks or the position that you received the offer for. Prer recommends, "Create a brag sheet. Keep a list of any wins that you have in your career. Everything! Even if you don't think that it is that big of a deal. This builds your inner confidence because you have it. This becomes your evidence sheet for a prospective employer."

Differentiators may include:

- Greater work experience
- More relevant work experience

- Professional certifications
- Advanced degrees

HAVE MULTIPLE LEVERS TO PULL

Negotiations are often about sharing and capturing information to make a better decision. Doing your research up front can help you have the conversation and determine which levers can be pulled. In any negotiation, you should consider your *best alternative to a negotiated agreement* (BATNA). In essence, this is the minimum that you are prepared to accept before you pursue another alternative. Having multiple options increases your bargaining power and ability to walk away. Having another offer gives you a benchmark and a stronger BATNA to leverage in your negotiation. There are also multiple levers beyond salary that you can prioritize and potentially pull to help sweeten the offer. Consider:

- Title, or path to a higher title (such as an advanced performance review that could lead to a higher title if certain expectations are met)
- Signing bonus
- Office location
- Start date
- Training (access to company training that may be limited to a certain number of people or the company paying for certain certifications or training)
- Benefits such as vacation days

Prer's advice is to

> . . . not be afraid of "No's." You might have a conversation with the recruiter and let them know the package you are after. They may say, "no" and then they may come back to you. Be aware that "no" is not a "no." Jobs are a match on both sides, and it is not about you trying to win over the other person. It has to be a match on both sides, and if it is not a match right now, it could mean another opportunity may be a better match. Don't be afraid to walk away if you don't get what you want!

Sharing information and learning what matters to your prospective employer can help you build a path to agreement and evaluate whether you are a match. While you may not be able to get the salary or title that you want right away, looking at the full menu can help you order the right options for a satisfying start to your career.

APPROACH AS A SHARED PROBLEM

Your prospective employer has given you an offer. They've invested a great deal of time evaluating numerous candidates, and you have made it through the gauntlet. Things have dramatically shifted from you wooing the company to the company wooing you. While your employer certainly has a BATNA as well (all of those people who did not receive offers), they don't want to lose you to a competitor or extend an offer to a lesser candidate. Both of you have a problem that you want to solve and the keys of information to help you unlock the offer. For instance, your prospective employer may have a closer start date in mind because they have already slated you for a project. This might be a high priority for you, and the firm may be willing to pay a premium for it. When you approach a negotiation from a zero-sum mindset, both sides tend to shield information and both sides lose to some extent.

All that being said, it is perfectly fine to use your own negotiating tactics. Anchor high with your benchmark and don't be impressed by the first offer. Remember that many companies leave some room for negotiation. Take time to review the offer thoroughly and compare it against other offers or benchmarks. When you do follow up, ask open-ended questions to collect information and also try to have conversations over the phone, digitally, or in person rather than doing a back-and-forth email exchange. With any negotiation, remain positive and polite, thank them for partnering with you on the conversation and continually bring the conversation back to the value that you will bring to the company. Prer Bania shares the importance of speaking up and letting your needs be known – especially for women! Prer's guidance:

> In general, for women, it is more about the aspect of speaking up and letting their needs be known. It goes back to being clear on what you actually need rather than what the other person will say "yes" to. I think this is where trust comes in and trust that an employer knows how to make a good decision for themselves and trust that if they have money budgeted, they will use that for a talented employee. Do not always base your next salary on your previous salary. Do not base your future salary based on what you are earning now. Base your salary on the value you bring!

> Approaching the negotiation from a state of "We both want me to end up at this company, let's figure out how we can make it happen" can open more doors and enable more levers to be pulled.

****

After nearly eight years with my former company, I began considering other opportunities. I had turned down several offers because ultimately, my BATNA at my former company was stronger and the other companies were unwilling to match what I was looking for. I stayed with my BATNA and with my former company. When I received an offer to join the team at Acumen Solutions (later acquired by Salesforce), I was excited by the prospect of working for an inspirational leader, organically growing the company, specializing in change management, and extending my craft through digital transformation efforts. When the initial offer came in, I was a bit underwhelmed – the title had been reduced along with compensation. They were also looking for a near-immediate start date. I was able to contact a friend who was working at a comparable company and show Acumen Solutions what the other company was offering candidates for a similar position. I shared where I stood from a career trajectory standpoint and where I exceeded the requirements in the job description and how this would translate into value for the company. Moreover, I put some additional cards on the table by highlighting that while I was willing to work with the start date, my daughter would be born soon, and I wanted time either before I started or soon after to spend with my growing family.

After I shared the benchmark information, the company was more willing to take a shared approach and review options. While I did not get everything on my menu, through information-sharing and openness, we were able to reach a compromise that left both of us satisfied. An hour of research and conversation led to significant movement from where we started, and both sides were able to reach an agreement. That hour of preparation, research, and conversation launched my career and opened my trajectory at this new company.

****

For further reading on negotiations, I highly recommend *Never Split the Difference*[3] by Chris Voss (a former hostage negotiator and a negotiations professor during my time at Georgetown's McDonough School of Business) and *Getting to Yes*[4] by Roger Fisher and William Ury, considered to be the quintessential book for negotiation.

15

WHY SHOULD YOU KEEP A CASE JOURNAL?

One of the best pieces of advice that I received was from case interview guru Marc Cosentino: Keep a case journal – a collection of current events, articles, and stories that you have come across that deal with a complex business challenge. My case journal was an invaluable asset during my MBA and is something that I have continued well after I landed a consulting job. It has enabled me to build creative solutions, adapt and apply business challenges, and use case studies as either benchmarks or cautionary tales about the risks a client faces. In your journal, you might record the source, the industry, and a quick overview of the challenge or takeaways from an article. Moreover, you might also consider key assumptions, supporting actions, or recommendations that come from a particular case or that you would have given had you been the consultant solving this business challenge.

Case journals can evolve over time to reflect the sophistication of your role. For instance, while I was initially looking at case studies, now I have added thought leadership and frameworks around managing teams, leadership principles, building relationships, and addressing strategic challenges to my case journal. As my library of knowledge articles grows, so does my toolkit and understanding as a consultant. There are three primary functions that a case journal serves: (1) building consulting muscles, (2) developing innovative solutions, and (3) extending your toolkit.

BUILDING CONSULTING MUSCLES

As an ongoing learner, you want to continue to acquire information that extends your knowledge and skills. A case journal enables you to capture content that you can regularly review, revisit, and apply to situations that you may experience as a consultant. Moreover, it gives you credibility in citing research, building analogies, and identifying novel ways of looking at problems. It helps you identify patterns and mold them for complex problems.

DEVELOPING INNOVATIVE SOLUTIONS

Consultants often look across industries for effective solutions and consider how these strategies can be adapted for an existing client or environment. While reinventing the wheel may be a waste of time, finding a new application for it can be a valuable innovation. In many instances, products, services, or strategies in one industry can be modified to fit another. Knowledge of these business cases and insights can enable you to build support for a recommendation, use a case study as a cautionary tale that galvanizes an executive to action, or create a halo effect by citing a credible organization as a paradigm for your solution.

EXTENDING YOUR TOOLKIT

Capturing ideas, concepts, and frameworks gives you more tools to apply to distinct situations. Whether managing a team, building a relationship with a client, or addressing a unique business challenge, a case journal enables you to have an increasing array of tools to apply and adapt. Extending your toolkit protects you from the old adage that when you only have a hammer, everything looks like a nail. You are able to look at problems more holistically, combine and adapt approaches, and reach a faster or more productive solution.

****

As you advance in your career, your case journal should be revisited. And while its content may evolve – or even *because* it evolves – it will continue to serve as an invaluable resource.

16

WHAT OBJECTIVES AND KEY RESULTS SHOULD YOU SET?

Business buzzword alert! Get used to speaking in acronyms and a different lexicon as part of consulting-speak. A question that I often get in various forms is, "What objectives and key results (OKRs) should you set early in your career?" OKRs are a framework for setting goals and tracking their results. Andy Grove, longtime CEO of Intel, was considered to be the founder of the OKR concept. This concept starts with an objective – a clearly defined goal – and three to five measurable outcomes that enable you to track progress toward that goal. Should you meet all of your OKRs? No. The recommended success rate for your objectives is 70%, which provides you with enough to work toward your objective while still stretching and allowing for growth. In the early stages of your career, I recommend setting OKRs around three key categories: (1) company/corporate contributions, (2) client delivery contributions, and (3) personal and professional development.

COMPANY/CORPORATE CONTRIBUTIONS: HOW ARE YOU CONTRIBUTING TO THE GROWTH OF THE FIRM?

There are a number of goals that you may set around corporate contributions and firm growth. Objectives in this area rest on three main pillars: (1) firm initiatives, (2) recruiting, and (3) business development.

Perhaps you want to contribute to firm initiatives. Your OKRs could center around building membership or attendance, number of activities or events, documents or materials produced, hours devoted to non-billable firm activity, amount of knowledge or lessons captured, and any initiative that you specifically led. Another opportunity to grow the firm is participating in recruiting events. Key results could include the number of people you connected with, the number of people you referred or interviewed, the number of hours you contributed to recruiting, the number of events attended, the number of coffee discussions with prospective consultants you held. With any of these, it is best to tie it back to results whenever possible – for example, how many of these candidates actually applied and were hired? Business development offers another opportunity to contribute to the firm growth. OKRs may include the number of proposals that you contributed to, the number of conferences attended, business development collateral developed, proposal capture rate, the number of dollars that you contributed to winning, the number of hours you spent on business development efforts, the roles that you played in proposals (showing increasing responsibility or diversifying skillset). Emphasizing results such as the total amount that you contributed to winning new prospects or clients generated will carry the most weight here.

CLIENT DELIVERY: HOW ARE YOU REPRESENTING THE FIRM WITH CLIENTS?

Client delivery takes precedence, and while your corporate contributions will become increasingly important as you progress, your priority should be supporting your project team and delivering stellar client results. Successful delivery often translates into a satisfied client, more business, and a project team that would like to work with you again. OKRs on the client delivery side may include meeting the project on time, within budget; testimonials, referrals, relationships built; or more business with that client. Key results on the project team side may include contributions to deliverables, added responsibilities, billable hours, contribution to project economics or project margins, and teammates willing to work with you again. Determining what the expectations are for the client and project team and then demonstrating how those expectations were exceeded can help you meet objectives and develop key results.

PERSONAL AND PROFESSIONAL DEVELOPMENT: HOW ARE YOU OWNING YOUR LEARNING AND GROWTH?

As you build your knowledge, skills, and abilities (KSAs), you become more valuable to the firm, project team, client, and industry. Objectives around personal and professional development may include contributions to your community, professional certifications earned, relevant coursework completed (internally within the firm and externally through other resources), and industry events attended. You can leverage the firm's resources to develop professionally and personally by joining affinity groups, taking part in trainings or brown bags, participating in firm networking events, and other activities. Key results could include the number of events or hours devoted to one of these activities, courses completed, skills and proficiency developed, certifications earned, and networking/coffee chats held. Externally, you may consider volunteer activities, conferences and industry events, and extracurriculars that enable you to build your KSAs. Similar to the internal OKRs, you may seek a target number of hours devoted to an activity, conferences or events attended, skills developed or proficiency level advanced, and how you have expanded your network.

****

While I did not necessarily think of the launch of my consulting career in terms of OKRs, I did set some tangible goals across each of these key areas. From the client delivery side, I sought to build relationships with the client and build our team (i.e., add business and revenue). I also sought to expand service and project offerings to the client while also meeting scope, time, and budget constraints. Additionally, I had target billable hours and project financials that I wanted to meet. On the firm side, I wanted to take part in and lead firm initiatives, including recruiting and onboarding. I also wanted to support the development of internal processes and to contribute to business development efforts by developing marketing material and writing proposals. Additionally, I wanted to mentor incoming members of the firm. From a professional development standpoint, I sought conferences and networking events to attend, set my sights on earning a project management professional (PMP) certification, and volunteered as a way to contribute more to my community.

Each of these unofficial OKRs would enable me to grow and would become goals in my performance review. Each year, I would build on my OKRs and my goals by taking on greater responsibility, earning additional professional certifications, and continuing to extend my community and company involvement.

17

HOW DO YOU IDENTIFY MENTORS?

No one achieves without someone else's help. I've had a number of people I considered as mentors and who have provided invaluable advice to me. Make sure that you have the right people in your corner providing the support that you need. Don't discount people because of age, experience, or field. Some of the best advice I ever received was from people junior to me who mentored up, and from people from different fields who shared cross-cutting experience. Recognize that mentoring is *something you both do* – it is proactive, takes work, and is bidirectional. To identify and find the right mentor(s): (1) be coachable, (2) be personable, and (3) define your goals.

BE COACHABLE: A MENTOR MAY FIND YOU

To make yourself coachable, showcase a willingness to learn and start to establish a track record of success. As marketing guru and author Ryan Holiday claims, "To develop a reputation as someone who is teachable, curious, motivated, talented, and above all, well-balanced and reliable, is the single best way to attract a mentor."

As you seek mentors, make sure you find people whom you respect, can build rapport with, and who may have built their careers on the foundation of great advice. While it helps to have someone in your company who can provide guidance on how to advance in the company and manage office politics, you can also benefit from mentors outside of the company who can provide an alternative perspective.

BE PERSONABLE: IT'S ABOUT BUILDING A RELATIONSHIP

Mentoring does not need to be formal. In fact, it often works better if the relationship is an informal professional connection. Get to know your mentor as a person and establish an authentic, rather than a transactional, relationship. Follow up regularly to provide updates and to learn what is happening in their life. Show that you value and appreciate their time and this relationship, and make sure to recognize and acknowledge the role that they play in your career and in your life. This will get your mentor more invested in your success and galvanize them to help you avoid business pitfalls, to serve as an advocate, and to connect you to opportunities.

DEFINE YOUR GOALS: DEVELOP YOUR ROADMAP

Fortunately, you now have built (or are building) your personal board of advisors and are developing your career strategic plan. These are essential factors in helping to identify a mentor. A mentor is someone you aspire to be, a better version of yourself. Knowing where you want to go can help you find someone to serve as a role model. Fundamentally, they share similar values about leadership and management, and may have had similar goals during the same stage of their careers. Be open with your mentor about your goals, and they may be able to provide insights into how to advance, prioritize actions, or help you align efforts.

****

Mentorship is about growth on both sides and can be mutually beneficial in advancing your career and your mentor's. Establishing a relationship where you can be candid, take constructive criticism and implement this feedback, and appreciate the advice will help you advance and build a model to pay it forward for aspiring consultants launching their careers. Because in the end, mentoring is about paying it forward. As you advance in your career, you may continue to learn from mentors, but you need to be a part of providing the support and advice that will help others.

18

HOW DO YOU IDENTIFY YOUR STRENGTHS?

You exert much less effort and get much better results by catering to your strengths rather than trying to buttress your weaknesses. Knowing your strengths is empowering and enables you to craft your career, roles, and opportunities around your unique talents. While there are a range of assessments to help you learn your strengths and how to activate them, the three that I have found most useful in my career are: (1) Clifton (Gallup) StrengthsFinder, (2) DISC Assessment, and (3) Goleman Leadership Style Assessment.

CLIFTON (GALLUP) STRENGTHS ASSESSMENT: KNOW YOUR TALENT DNA

Self-awareness is such an important part of consulting. Building relationships with skeptical clients, working across diverse teams, and navigating projects and opportunities at your firm employ different skills. The Clifton Strengths Assessment measures your specific order of strengths across 34 themes and provides you with a personalized report of how you can best leverage these strengths. The assessment claims that users are six times as likely to be engaged in their jobs, six times as likely to strongly agree that they have the opportunity to do what they are best at, and three times as likely to report having an excellent quality of life.

The Strengths Assessment was illuminating for me in that it showed me my five core strengths – Achiever, Communication, Focus, Learner, Strategic. This knowledge helped me start to craft roles, projects, and experiences around these strengths. Moreover, as I considered other job opportunities, it enabled me to ask better questions about roles and weed out prospects that did not align with my strong points. While you can certainly be successful in jobs that don't use your strengths, it takes far more time and effort than finding a role that is more naturally linked to them.

DISC ASSESSMENT: LEARN YOUR BEHAVIORAL TENDENCIES

The DISC assessment is one of the world's most popular behavioral assessments. Knowing your behavioral style, as well as being able to evaluate the behavioral style of others, enables you to better utilize the appropriate communication techniques in your interactions with that particular person. Moreover, it helps you to use awareness of your own behavioral tendencies and to moderate or adapt to these tendencies. The assessment helps you to identify characteristics of each of the four tendencies:

- **Dominance:** Assertive, results-focused, rapid decisions; can be aggressive and desires to lead
- **Influence:** Outgoing and persuasive, people-oriented, optimistic; has strong communication skills
- **Steadiness:** Patient and prefers stability and structure; operates at a deliberate pace
- **Conscientious:** Analytical and fact-based; follows structure and abides by rules

As a consultant, you will undoubtedly be in situations where you need to work across different styles, persuade clients, and develop business. Knowing your own style, as well as qualifying the style of those you interact with, can help you vary your communications approaches to increase success.

I've found this tool particularly helpful for qualifying clients. Identifying their style enables you to build more effective recommendations, presentations, and relationships. For instance, knowing that you have a client who tends toward steadiness means that you may want to establish regular progress checks, incorporate their feedback, and highlight the risks of not doing something in order to usher them along.

GOLEMAN LEADERSHIP STYLE ASSESSMENT: IDENTIFY YOUR APPROACH AND BLIND SPOTS

While not as well-known as the two assessments I've mentioned above, the Goleman Leadership Style Assessment ties that all-too-critical element of emotional intelligence into how you work with and lead teams. As someone who will need to lead in a variety of different situations with a diverse group of people, it is extremely important to know your leadership style. This assessment identifies six core leadership styles and provides you with an understanding of the strengths of each style as well as potential blind spots that could inhibit your abilities to work in, and lead, a team. The six leadership styles are:

- Coercive (commanding)
- Pace-setting
- Authoritative
- Affiliative
- Democratic
- Coaching

When I took this assessment in business school, I found it to be one of the most influential and informative of any I had taken. It was not entirely surprising that I was a "pace-setter" (that is, I am constantly trying to set the tone, push the boundaries, and lead the team to greater achievement). I was a little more surprised to discover my blind spots. While being a pace-setter can lead to high-performing teams, it also runs the risk of burnout. Pace-setters are "obsessive about doing things faster or better," which not only can lead to low morale, but also can cause people to feel like they are failing if they cannot keep pace. Knowing my blind spots enabled me to better adjust my leadership style – to set regular checkpoints and remind myself to meet people where they are.

****

Knowing your strengths, behavioral tendencies, and leadership styles (and knowing the characteristics of other types) can help you qualify and adapt your own approach, seek opportunities that cater to your strengths, and recognize and mitigate your blind spots. Being aware of others' working styles can also help you to adapt your communications, approaches, and strategies to help more effectively lead a team and achieve better results.

19

HOW DO YOU BE A GREAT TEAMMATE?

A big part of consulting is teamwork. Often, you are working under tight deadlines with a group whose members have varying strengths, skill sets, and experiences, and the team needs to self-organize their skills, time, and responsibilities to best address a challenge. Good teammates create advocates who keep wanting to work with them again and will actively seek them out for projects. Indeed, some consulting firms have even added questions around teammates in their year-end performance reviews: (1) Would you want to work with this person again? and (2) Would you be willing to sacrifice part of your bonus to this person based on their performance? Keeping this in mind, being a good teammate not only is the right thing to do, it can positively impact your career trajectory by fostering lasting relationships and getting you placed on important projects, which can lead to financial reward as well. Being a good teammate requires listening, so I've developed an acronym to remind you of attributes of a good teammate. HEAR what your team is saying through their words, actions, and body language by *helping, empathizing, anticipating*, and *recognizing*.

HELPING: THE LITTLE THINGS MATTER

When you work with a team, find ways to contribute and adapt your time and skills to the situation. If you finish your aspect of the project early, offer to help others. Coach others and help them build their skills. Share best practices or practices that have helped make you more effective. This creates a culture of collaboration and can foster a flywheel of support. Even little things, like offering to pick up a cup of coffee for others as you go to get one for yourself, can signal your willingness to support the team. Make yourself available to help others and do not just operate within the confines of your piece of the project.

Tiffany Yang was one of the best teammates that I ever had. She did all of the little things and made my job managing a team much easier. Even though our team has gone their separate ways, the bonds we built continue to grow.

We keep in touch, are invested in each other's success, and still have our inside jokes and memories of our time in the consulting trenches. Tiffany shared one aspect that makes teams great:

> Teammates bring their best, and their team can expect them to know (and vocalize) when they need to take a break to recalibrate. Time off to take care of personal appointments and needs decreases individual stress and reaffirms that their team is present to provide support when they need it. And, when (not if) team members are having a tough day or going through difficult life circumstances, space, empathy, and understanding allow them to return with a clear head, versus lashing out at teammates or ignoring an issue and allowing it to persist, interfering with their ability to work. Teammates who give each other time graciously will find that, rather than abusing it, devoted teammates will want to do the same for others.

The little things matter – and know when your teammate could use a little extra.

EMPATHIZING: GET TO KNOW TEAMMATES ON A PERSONAL LEVEL

Seek to understand your teammates and get to know where they are coming from. While work styles and work strengths are important, perhaps even more important are the relationships. Be mindful of the signals of when a teammate is stressed or operating under a lot of pressure. Milestones matter – not just on the project, but also in life. Be aware of what is going on outside your teammates' work environment and how it is affecting them. Know when they have life milestones on the horizon – birthdays, weddings, children – and (if the person is comfortable with it) get the team involved in celebrating.

When I was on a project for a challenging client, one of the best teams that I had ever worked on had aced the art of empathy. Someone, without fail, would know when a major life milestone was coming for a member of the team and organize a mini celebration for birthdays or housewarming gifts or a baby shower. This did not take a lot of additional effort and it paid dividends in our team culture. The person we were celebrating not only appreciated the life recognition, they also became more willing to go above and beyond, working harder and collaborating with the team. More than three years after that team started to dissolve for different roles and projects, we still keep in touch, support each other, and update each other on life's milestones. Who knows? We may even reunite down the road as we start other projects, join other firms, or build other teams.

Tiffany was a major contributor to our team and highlighted the rapport that this team had built:

> The team was really invested in our individual and collective success. There was no shortage of support when it came to personal hobbies, professional growth, and team building. Members provided support by giving time and money to others' causes, being non-judgmental when offering/providing support (e.g., hosting one-on-one sessions or brown bags to teach a skill, covering for a teammate who was taking leave to *do x*, etc.), and genuinely listening with curiosity about another teammate's interest. The team recognized the importance of support and growth for individuals and for the group.

Thirty-plus percent of your day is at work, so build relationships and teams that make that time well spent.

ANTICIPATING: SOLVE THE ISSUE BEFORE IT BECOMES A PROBLEM

Good teammates anticipate by sharing their perspective and offering suggestions to mitigate risks, build relationships, and address team and client needs. Having a teammate who looks ahead and produces something to help the team even before the team knows it is needed enables the team to build trust. This leads the team to perform at a higher level. When I have a teammate who anticipates an issue and comes prepared with a solution, or who has an idea on how we can do something better and shares that idea, I not only feel gratitude, but also feel a sense of camaraderie. That person has my and the team's back and I can trust them to think through what will make us more effective.

This happened recently on a project that was just launching. We were building relationships with key stakeholders and highlighting our efforts and progress. We had not directly shared updates with one very important member of the project team who was a big advocate of our work (and whom we wanted to continue to be an advocate). A teammate quickly drafted an email highlighting what we had accomplished to date and where we would welcome this stakeholder's feedback and shared this with me. While this was a seemingly minor action, it showed that they were thinking holistically about how to improve our performance, effectiveness, and relationships.

Moreover, it had the anticipated effect by building a stronger relationship with this stakeholder.

Tiffany Yang was extra adept at anticipating the team's needs, and this fostered a virtuous cycle. By anticipating the needs of the team, others would follow suit. As Tiffany describes it,

> Another outcome of working on a good team was continuous progress. We all knew what our objectives were, and we continuously worked to hit project milestones, advance stakeholder relationships, and keep long-term goals in sight. Because we agreed on objectives, we continuously moved forward with the same external messaging— because we knew where we were going, those around us did, too.

RECOGNIZING: GIVE CREDIT WHERE IT IS DUE

Good teammates recognize each other's efforts and contributions. They show appreciation and gratitude for the attention to detail, added effort, or extra time that a teammate devoted to the project. Recognition is often the easiest and least expensive way to build rapport, foster trust, and show value. When teammates know their work is valued, it increases productivity, satisfaction, and motivation. Giving credit for solid work can create a virtuous cycle of recognition, camaraderie, and effectiveness.

One project that I joined midstream (when it was already well under way) was facing severe morale issues. Teammates were siloed, had their heads down working overtime on their pieces of the project, and often failed to consider the interdependencies of their contributions to the project. The team was frustrated, burned out, and not always willing to devote their time to help others. This started to change as I acknowledged and recognized people for their efforts. I would thank the team for contributions they made to my piece of the project and time that they shared with me. I acknowledged that people were working nights and weekends to get things done and that their hour or so helping me had a multiplier on what I was able to accomplish. Gradually, I began to receive more support and teammates became more willing to share their time and expertise with each other. Without that, we would have drastically failed on this effort.

****

Tiffany Yang shared her perspective on strong teams: "Great team moments are built on many, many smaller wins." Help build those moments! Being a good teammate requires listening to what is said and unsaid and HEARing your teammates.

20

WHAT DO YOU LOOK FOR IN A CONSULTING PROJECT?

There are a number of factors to weigh when getting placed into or targeting your next project. Being aware of them can help you evaluate potential projects and position yourself for career-defining opportunities. The five factors that I typically consider when evaluating a consulting project are: (1) team, (2) expertise, (3) account growth prospects, (4) measurability, and (5) stability. While these are not the only points to look at, and many may not fall within your locus of control as a relatively junior consultant, they can help you aim for successful, high-visibility projects. Note that these five factors conveniently spell out TEAMS – the most important quality to consider.

TEAM: WORKING TOGETHER TO ACCOMPLISH A SHARED GOAL

For me, the team is almost always the most important factor when considering a project. A team that supports each other, identifies and utilizes core strengths, and integrates and aligns efforts to meet the client's demands makes the experience much more meaningful and the project much more likely to succeed. A poor team environment, where the members operate in silos, look out for themselves, and focus on individual contributions rather than the success of the team not only leads to a challenging climate, but also leads to lower prospects for success, higher stress, and less likelihood that you will walk away from the project with advocates.

When considering a team, look at who will be leading the project and what their track record is. Does this person have a reputation for building a solid team? Leveraging people's strengths? Coaching and empathizing? Completing projects on time and within budget, and satisfying the client?

Look at the team members' skills and experiences. Are there people who you can learn from? Is there a role that you can play or a strength that you can add to the team? Do teammates have a solid reputation in the firm?

Finally, consider the client. Often, you will be collaborating with and crafting solutions for the client. Does the client provide feedback and input and are they a regular part of the review process? Does the client understand the scope of the project and stay aligned with that scope? Does the client communicate with the project team when there is an issue? Is the client supportive of the project? Doubtful about it? Straight-up against it?

Tiffany Yang shared her insights from her team experience and what she modeled being an excellent teammate:

> Teams produce exceptional results when all members feel supported and heard. Each team member brings different strengths and perspectives, but this diversity is null if team members aren't given space to show, apply, and learn from them with their teams. Though it's impossible to include each person's opinion into every decision, it's hugely important to ensure that teams provide a venue for collective discussion so that all members feel that they are continuously contributing to the group's success.

A challenging team environment can yield lessons that help you grow as a consultant and team leader. Strive to be a part of a team where there is a culture of collaboration, cohesion, and combining of skills and contributions are recognized.

EXPERTISE: BUILD DISTINGUISHING SKILLS AND EXPERIENCES

Evaluate the role that you would play on the project and what expertise you'd bring to it. If you'd be playing a heavy data role and that is not your core strength, then are you really best positioned to fill that role? If the role requires using strong design skills to develop presentations, and that is something that you avoid on project teams, is it the right role for you? There is something to be said for taking on challenging roles and responsibilities and developing or strengthening skills. This is how consultants learn, grow, and achieve. However, as you begin your career, I often advise playing to your strengths and gradually learning from others on your teams. When you consider a project, assess the role, what expertise the team needs, and what experience you will develop from your time on the project. Take calculated risks. What is the gap between your experience and the role? Do you have time or the ability to quickly fill that gap? Will the experience you gain make you a stronger consultant? Will the experience that you gain be valued by the firm? Some projects may offer experiences that position you as a unique contributor in the firm or give you the opportunity to specialize. While this can be valuable for your initial growth, specialization runs the risk of you getting pigeonholed into certain projects or clients. Consider the short-term trade-offs and build these into your career planning and 3–5 year plan.

ACCOUNT GROWTH PROSPECTS: DEVELOP BUSINESS AND ALIGN TO ACCOUNT GROWTH

A growing account reflects well on the project team and, by extension, those contributing to the team. This shows that the team has succeeded in building relationships, providing the client with satisfactory work, and extending the company's brand and reputation with the client. Moreover, being a part of this team enables you to take part in or observe business development efforts and contribute to the overall growth of the account. An account primed for growth opens opportunities, enables you to more actively participate in business development efforts, and allows you to link some of your efforts to the account growth. While account growth may not always be easy to forecast, there are signs that you may be able to follow:

- Has the client worked with your firm in the past, and have these efforts been successful?
- Has the client extended contracts beyond their initial terms?
- Has the firm won additional work?
- Is the client considering other projects aligned with your firm's expertise?
- Has your firm developed strong relationships with the client?
- Does there seem to be a natural progression to the work that is not included in the current contract?

Consider the answers to these questions as you review account growth prospects and evaluate the role that you can play in these efforts.

MEASURABILITY: DETERMINE PROJECT VISIBILITY

First, let's clarify – visibility should be positive. You'd like to avoid projects that are one fire drill after another, where client demands are shifting, profitability is low as costs and personnel are added, hours are being burned to address issues, and timelines are extended beyond what was initially planned. That being said, these challenging projects can also provide an opportunity to shine by learning from and addressing these obstacles head on. Understand how your firm measures projects and what they deem a successful project. Typically, project economics include such quantitative factors as:

- **Profitability:** The revenue earned minus the costs to provide the services. The project is delivered on a budget and within a certain profitability range.
- **Time:** The time planned for the project against the actual time to complete the project. It is delivered on time.
- **Client Satisfaction:** The project meets the client's expectations of quality, which translates into referrals, testimonials, positive statements, and ongoing or future business from the client.

Several qualitative factors could enhance visibility. For instance, the effort may be led by a rising star – who has a halo effect on the project. The effort could also be around a current hot topic with the client getting positive press for their efforts or being recognized for leadership, innovation, products, or services. Working with a high-profile and successful client could also increase your firm's visibility and your visibility inside the firm. Learn how your firm evaluates project success and better understand how prospective projects forecast to these metrics. As you become more adept at understanding project economics and success metrics, you will also become better at identifying project risks that could hinder performance.

STABILITY: QUALIFYING QUALITY OF LIFE

One factor that you should not overlook is the impact that this project could have on your quality of life and work-life balance. Will the project require frequent travel? If so, how far will you be traveling? Will the project require work hour adjustments? How easy will it be to adhere to those adjustments? Does the project look overly ambitious? Do you anticipate some late nights and weekends (and are you comfortable with that)? While a great part of your project hygiene (your project quality of life) depends on the team, there are certain project hygiene factors that you can assess up front:

- Commute time
- Deliverable schedule
- Project expectations (availability, billable hours, role)
- Travel frequency and commute time
- Work hours (expect to adapt if you are working across time zones)

****

Ultimately, consultants do not always get to choose their clients and, depending on the firm, may have little say in their projects. Being aware of the five factors above helps you to potentially influence where you land on a project or begin to position yourself for projects that rank high on these factors. Moreover, you can evaluate and plan for projects that may rank low but will enable you to develop a plan to craft opportunities elsewhere in the firm. For instance, if you are on a low-growth project, you may be able to identify business development opportunities that are related to the industry or type of service that you are offering and contribute elsewhere. If you know that you will be traveling frequently or will need to adjust your work hours for the client or project team, you can begin making changes now. For instance, you might outsource some of your errands (dry cleaning, limit grocery shopping) or plan how travel will impact your personal or social life and schedule things around your hours or travel. Getting on a project that does not cater to your strengths, has a struggling manager, or that is low growth does not doom your career by any means. Take time to learn from these challenges, reflect on mistakes and their outcomes, and build skills that make you more successful on your next less-than-ideal project.

When I asked Rohit Agarwal, who had been a senior engagement manager at McKinsey, about what he looked for in a project, he told me,

> Ask yourself, What are you uniquely good at? What is your superpower? How do you create more opportunities to do work along your strengths? There are a number of high-leverage points where some meetings, presentations, and projects are more valuable to your development and career trajectory. For many people, it will depend on your staffing model. The number-one factor in my opinion is the manager. I was fortunate in that I was often very aligned with my manager, and it is extremely important that you can see yourself working closely with this group of people. Is the leadership going to take time to invest in you? People get busy, and are they going to take the time to coach you and present you with opportunities to stretch yourself? This is hard to know when you join, and the best way to know this is by talking to other people in the firm about which managers take the time to do this. The second thing is content – people are more passionate when they are working on things that they care about. The third part is function – which skills are you building? Far and away, having a manager who is

invested in your career is the most important factor.

Recently, I was assigned to a project overseas that required frequent travel – two weeks on and two weeks off of the client site. With a five-month-old and my wife returning to work, we discussed the project and the impact it would have on our family. While it was an exciting and highly visible project, the time away from family and the sacrifices that my wife would have to make were too much. We offered alternatives (traveling less frequently or returning home on weekends), but unfortunately, those alternatives were not possible. COVID would ultimately change the travel expectations, and I was able to join the project later. My wife and I had to adapt our schedules because the client started six hours ahead of my time zone and the team would be working across seven time zones. Knowing this up front enabled me to better prepare and adapt my schedule so that I could contribute to a successful project.

21

WHAT DO YOU DO IF A PROJECT DOES NOT ALIGN WITH YOUR VALUES?

When I was presenting at Carnegie Mellon's Heinz College of Information Systems and Public Policy, a question quickly turned into a discussion on how to craft and navigate your career. As we walked through a case that focused on helping a client develop a recruitment and retention strategy for border patrol agents (based on a Government Accountability Office report), many people cringed as we discussed the client's mission in the context of today's political landscape. A very valid question was raised: "How do you work for a client when you do not agree with how they are carrying out their mission?"

This is a robust topic, and one that you could face in many industries. Marketing firms do not always choose their clients (they may find themselves hired by "vice industries" like alcohol, gambling, or firearms), and consulting companies may rationalize serving a controversial client in the name of impact, revenue, service expansion, or various other reasons. Your approach to controversial projects may impact your career choices – which firms to target, which relationships to make, which projects to take.

CONSIDER A RANGE OF RESPONSES

In consulting, you don't always get to choose your clients. Many companies may place you on whichever project is readily available; other projects may be assigned if there is a match between your skills and the project's needs (independent of the client or industry). You'll need to weigh a lot of factors as you navigate your early consulting engagements and position yourself for adding value to the client and company. You may factor in the relationships you've built with senior leaders in the firm, the opportunity for career advancement, the growth opportunity that comes with working with a controversial client, or the ability to have an impact. If you are concerned with being placed on a project that does not align with your values, here are six potential responses that you could receive from your firm:

- **Preference Considered:** The company recognizes that you have experience, preferences, or clients that are better aligned with your passions and works with you to try to make sure you are placed on a project that is aligned with your values and where you can do your best work.
- **Seat at the Table:** The company shares that working for a controversial client gives you a seat at the table to engage, open dialogue, and potentially affect change. Clients hire consultants for an "outside perspective," and you might provide an alternative and independent perspective that enables the client to shift their approach. The company would prefer that you stay with the controversial client.
- **Career Advancement:** The company acknowledges that the client is operating in a challenging industry or challenging political environment. The relationships you build, knowledge you gain, and experience you develop working with a controversial client will help you advance with the firm. The company would prefer that you to stay with the controversial client.
- **Career Opportunity:** While the client may not be attractive to you, it is one that the firm is providing services for. The company leadership may feel that all clients are entitled to services. Just as lawyers provide services to clients they may not agree with, the company is a professional services firm that provides a service to a client in need. Taking on a controversial client can help you build relationships and deliver work that can add more value to the firm. The company would prefer that you stay with the controversial client.
- **Try It Out:** The company and client could use your insights on this project and the client could benefit from your perspective. This will enable you to be billable and gain valuable experience. The company would like you to test it out for a designated period of time and then reevaluate with an advisor.
- **In or Out:** The company has set billable targets expectations, and this project is readily available. If you want to meet company expectations, you'll need to work with that client and meet your targets.

These responses range from the more collaborative ("Let's work with you on this") to the more draconian ("Are you part of the team or not?"). Being aware of these potential responses can help you evaluate firms' culture and prospective engagements. Note that the onus is on you to initiate this conversation, so make sure to do your research on the project, the client, and the company's role before you do.

RESEARCH BEFORE YOU COMMIT

When evaluating a firm, you will need to consider whether they reflect your values and whether they are willing to turn down potentially lucrative contracts and revenue to demonstrate those values. With data often publicly available, you can research firms and better understand what clients are in their portfolio. Before joining a company, conducting your due diligence is an obvious step. Research how the company segments their industries, which clients they support, and what projects they work on. Walk into your interview educated on clients that the company serves.

During your interview, you want to get a sense for the company's culture. Many companies will tout "people first," "integrity," and "exceptional client value," and you will want to clarify what these values mean in practice. Does "people first" mean allowing consultants to grow with clients whose missions address areas that they are passionate about? Does the company show its "integrity" by dropping clients when their values do not align with their values or if a client does not respect the consulting team? Is revenue the predominant factor for "exceptional client value"? Here are a few ways you can probe this during your interview:

- "Your company has a broad portfolio of projects and clients that provides a number of great opportunities for gaining experience across disciplines and industries. What factors do you consider when placing someone on a project?"
- "As someone with a strong background in X, I've noticed that you provide service to the Department of X. Would I be more likely to be placed on a Department of X project given my background and interest in X?"
- "While 'exceptional client service' is one of your core values, have you ever dropped a client because you felt that your values were misaligned or that you were unable to provide the service that the client demanded?"

The company's presence in an industry and factors that they consider in placing someone on a project can help you make a more informed decision about your likelihood of being placed on an engagement that does not align with your values and the response that the company may give if you push back at being placed on a controversial client. While consulting firms value diverse backgrounds and industry experience, they may not always factor your prior industry experience into client placement. Keep this in mind if you want to focus on a particular industry.

Consulting companies have a profit incentive. But some may be willing to take a stand and drop clients whose missions and values misalign with their employees' values. If a company can provide examples of when they dropped a client and provide the rationale, that may help you make a better-informed decision on how they address controversial clients. And in the interview, your goal is to build relationships, learn whether you and the company are a cultural fit, and to receive an offer. It is important to listen with an open mind, be politically agnostic, and ask questions that show that you have done your research and that will help you gain information to better evaluate your fit with the firm. Once you receive an offer, you will better be able to compromise, negotiate, and position yourself for a project.

TRADING REVENUE FOR VALUES?

Immigration and Customs Enforcement (ICE) has been the target of public outcry across the political spectrum for its enforcement of the Trump administration's "zero tolerance" policy on illegal immigration that led to the separation of children from their parents. The agency has also received a lot of criticism for its management of detention centers across the country.

McKinsey & Company had a contract for "management consulting services" in ICE's Enforcement and Removal Operations Division. According to a *New York Times*[5] report, the contract was awarded during the Obama administration, but most of the $20 million in consulting work was completed during the Trump administration. Employees and alumni raised concerns about the nature of the firm's role, prompting the contract to be modified and a managing partner to step forward and issue a statement that McKinsey would "not, under any circumstances, engage in any work, anywhere in the world, that advances or assists policies that are at odds with our values." According to public records, at least three other large consulting firms – Deloitte Consulting, Guidehouse (formerly PricewaterhouseCoopers), and Booz Allen Hamilton have advised ICE. A spokesman for Booz Allen Hamilton affirmed that the nature of the work involved "information systems, data integration, and analytics," and did not involve "the separation of children from adults." According to the *Popular Information*[6] newsletter, Deloitte has won over $104 million in contracts with ICE since the start of the Trump administration and $177 million in contracts with Customs and

Border Protection (CBP) since January 2017. The public and many of these firms' employees have called for greater scrutiny of the role these companies have played in providing services to ICE and CBP.

As a prospective employee, learning about a firm's client portfolio, governance processes, and project engagement approach can help you better understand where a company draws a line between revenue and values and whether you could end up providing services to a client that causes you to consider compromising your own values.

POSITION YOURSELF FOR AN INDUSTRY

The goal of the interview is to build relationships, learn more about the company, and receive an offer. Once you have received an offer, you are in a better position to negotiate. The company invested time in recruiting and selecting you and have laid their cards on the table and let you know that they want you to join the team. They do not know if you feel the same or are possibly weighing another offer. If client placement was left ambiguous during your interview, you are in a better position to raise concerns with the client portfolio, project placement, and set parameters after you receive an offer.

For instance, if you have not already connected with a leader in a target industry, you can ask to speak or meet with practice leaders in a target industry before you make a decision. This will enable you to start building relationships, learn more about the nature of the work, and identify opportunities for project placement. You may also want to connect with practice leaders in industries where you have concerns so that you can better understand the nature of those portfolios and test your assumptions. Doing so allows you to see if the firm values your opinions and concerns and enables you to build a network and relationships within an industry that you are passionate about.

WHERE DO YOU DRAW THE LINE?

In a conversation with a manager at a large consulting firm who is leading a project with a "controversial" client, he talked about how he views this question:

> There are a number of different aspects to it – the company, the manager, and the individual. Companies often do a lot to review how they are contributing to the mission of an organization. Many companies will

not get involved in an organization where their values are misaligned or will seek work with that organization that avoids controversial areas. Many consulting firms may look to get involved in how to support the mission without it touching an area that is controversial. You need to recognize where a company is putting their values and where they are drawing their line. You should be in agreement with the company on ethical lines, and I would encourage people to have conversations with leadership to determine where they draw the line.

There is also a recognition that this is client service and clients deserve representation. If you have any issues with a particular client and if you have any obstacles that prevent you from doing your best work for a client and company, then you should communicate that to your manager and move yourself to a better situation. You can manage the situation responsibly and should feel comfortable sharing your concerns and educating yourself on the company's rationale for working with a particular client. I've seen a lot of younger consultants who protest, submit a petition, and escalate something to firm leadership rather than capturing the full scope and knowing the facts. This can harm your reputation within the firm. There are times and places where you will have to stand up to your company. Know who you are working for, trust the company will have a conversation with you, and have a conversation about how you can do the best work for the clients that you serve.

The manager noted the importance of doing your due diligence, initiating the conversation, and entering the conversation with an open mind.

Ultimately, you need to capture information, test your assumptions, and determine where you personally draw the line about the clients or issues the company takes on. Even if you do not believe in how a client organization is carrying out its mission, do you believe that it is entitled to professional services? Do you believe that this mission is going to be carried out regardless and that providing consulting services can save taxpayer dollars (in the social sector) and provide safer conditions for the client's employees on the front lines? Do you believe that having a seat at the table and providing your perspective could raise valuable points that an organization may not be considering? Would you be willing to work for a controversial organization supporting a project in an area that is sectioned off from the controversy? Or do you place a premium on values and are you unwilling to work for a company that provides any support to an organization that you feel is carrying out harmful policies or providing harmful services or products? Conducting due diligence and establishing your own internal litmus test will help you prioritize the companies that you target.

22

HOW DO YOU OVERCOME TEAM CONFLICT?

Since its inception, IBM has been regarded as an innovative and evolving company. Big Blue's ability to anticipate and adapt to conflict has contributed to the company's longevity and success. In the 1990s, IBM bundled products and reintegrated divisions in an effort to provide customers with fuller products and services. This transition, outlined in the *Harvard Business Review* article "Want Collaboration? Accept – and Actively Manage – Conflict,"[7] fostered greater complexity and conflict within sales and delivery, as well as between previously independent divisions. Managers were escalating or not addressing conflicts across units, leading to a loss of service and the erosion of competitive advantages that had taken IBM decades to forge. Without greater accountability and communication, the company would continue to suffer losses in market share and customer satisfaction. It recognized that setting and communicating expectations and collaborating across units was critical to resolving conflicts. The company developed the Market Growth Workshop, which brought managers, salespeople, and frontline specialists together to identify, discuss, and develop action steps to address conflicts across business units. The company developed a simple template that clarified expectations and forced people to document and assess issues discussed during the workshop. Documenting, tracking, and clarifying these issues helped to hold people accountable and manage expectations. What could have been a catastrophic spiral of coalitions between silos, finger-pointing, and selling of business units ultimately became a way for IBM leaders to communicate, take action, and use processes and personnel to address high-stakes and highly visible conflicts. *Forbes* has ranked IBM as one of the world's most valuable brands (24th on its 2020 list of "*The World's Most Valuable Brands*").

EMBRACE THE INEVITABLE: WORKING WITH CONFLICT

Conflict an inevitable part of the work environment. And in today's firms, generational differences, tight deadlines, and the need for getting more done with less have only ratcheted up the tensions that can lead to strife. Many people naturally attempt to handle conflict by avoiding it. It's unpleasant and may likely add even more stress to a stressful situation. We also have an innate desire to be liked, which strengthens our tendency to avoid conflict. Yet while sidestepping conflict may seem desirable, this tactic is not always constructive.

Think of the person who repeatedly turns in work past deadlines. While not addressing this conflict up front may enable you to avoid unpleasant interactions, it lowers team morale, particularly of those who are working overtime to play catch-up. It also enables the slacking coworker to continue to turn in work late, which continues the cycle of resentment and extra work. And it adds strain to the project manager, who cannot rely on deadlines being met.

Instead of allowing such situations to arise, teammates need to face conflict head-on. To do so, they need not only to be able to identify the type of conflict that has arisen, but also have a toolkit of techniques to mitigate, address, and harness it.

DEFINING CONFLICT: KNOW THE WARNING SIGNALS

Merriam-Webster's Dictionary defines "conflict" as "mental struggle resulting from incompatible or opposing needs, drives, wishes, or external or internal demands."[8] Note the key phrase "mental struggle" – conflict occupies our minds and impacts our well-being. Allowed to fester, it damages a team's morale and effectiveness. Here are just a few ways conflict can harm a team:

- Lower productivity
- Increased stress
- Frustration due to time lost to address conflict
- Reduced trust
- "With us or against us" mentality
- Win/lose mentality (someone wins while someone loses)
- Lose/nose mentality (no one wins)

Conflict can hinder efforts, damage relationships, and lower productivity when warning signals are not identified and project leaders do not effectively channel these warning signals into productive dialogue.

However, when project leaders or teams do recognize the signs, conflict can be productive. In an interview with Eric Williamson, a conflict management expert and author of *How to Work with Jerks*,[9] he highlights that conflict has the potential to be a net positive for your team if managed appropriately: "Conflict is generally a good thing because it represents an opportunity to improve. It can also encourage new thinking and different perspectives. It creates an opportunity for people to be more empathetic as well as see things from someone else's point of view. Instead of focusing on being right, it can allow us to focus on doing the right thing—which may involve putting yourself in someone else's shoes and seeing things from their perspective." For instance, handled the right way, conflict can:

- Energize teams
- Increase creativity
- Encourage stronger communication and emotional intelligence skills
- Enhance negotiations
- Lead to questions unlocking better solutions
- Discover others' perspectives, needs, and values

To foster productive conflict, consultants must be adept at reading personalities, assessing situations, and using a range of tools and techniques to prevent conflict from metastasizing into a toxic situation.

ASSESSING CONFLICT: CHANNELING CONFLICT INTO HEALTHY RESULTS

The extent to which conflict will impact the project often depends on the personalities and degree to which the friction has grown. Conflict tends to follow a life cycle, and addressing it in the early stages often leads to a higher ability and willingness of all parties to reach a win/win resolution. Conflict might start small. People mask their negative emotions and feelings and will likely seek win/win resolutions, have mutual respect for the other participants, and be willing to reach a resolution before conflict escalates. Additionally, at this stage, many people have not become entrenched in their opinions, deadlines may be further away, and there is less pressure to reach a resolution. Teams should attempt to instill a culture where issues are discussed openly, perspectives are shared, and positions are not hardened. For instance, removing ambiguity by explicitly setting and documenting deadlines and expectations is one way to ensure communication and clarify needs.

As conflict evolves, it becomes important to identify the initial warning signals – hardening positions, intense debates, and the forming of coalitions – in order to mitigate it before it becomes full-blown. As emotions intensify, debates become more bitter, it becomes more difficult to use words to reach a compromise, and coalitions solidify. In these stages, conflict becomes win/lose as one side looks to gain at the expense of the other. It is important during meetings to take minutes or notes and review them, as well as document requests and timelines in email so that there is a paper trail where expectations can be reviewed and revisited.

When conflict reaches its peak, participants take a lose/lose approach by seeking victory at all costs. At this stage, discussions break down, threats are made, people are clearly divided, and the conflict might end in a complete impasse or breakup. Teams must adeptly redirect conflict at this stage or face a war of attrition. Being aware of the warning signals of unproductive conflict can help you de-escalate conversations and channel conflict to more productive outcomes:

- Emotions dominate the facts
- Fear and mistrust increase
- Perspective is one-sided, no middle ground
- Information is restricted
- Solutions are not based in logic
- People shut down, do not participate in conversations

Teams must actively monitor conflict to ensure that disagreement remains productive and does not spiral into all-out war.

MANAGING CONFLICT: STRATEGIES FOR SUCCESS

As you go through the conflict life cycle, be mindful of the personalities involved and the approaches that can be used depending on who is involved and the situation. Below are several approaches that have been adapted from the Management and Strategy Institute, along with when they tend to successfully work and when they might exacerbate the situation:

APPROACH	SUCCESSFUL WHEN...	POTENTIALLY BACKFIRES WHEN...
Accommodation	• Dissenters care little about the outcome • Dissenters are wrong • Dissenters have little power	• Dissenters resent position afterward • Dissenters appear weak • It makes others appear strong
Avoidance	• Time is short • Dissenters have less power • Relationship has no value to dissenters • Dissenters desire to block progress • Issue is trivial	• Team members care about the relationship • Used repeatedly • Creates a future expectation • Harms image
Collaboration	• Sides desire to preserve relationship • Critical to reach ideal solution • Sides prefer to cooperate as a strategy • All issues can be addressed • A win/win outcome is needed	• Ethical or moral issues • Time sensitive issue • Trivial issue • Irresolvable/ irreconcilable differences • No mutual respect
Compromise	• A nonoptimal solution is OK • Time and resources are limited • Sides have equal power • Only way to a win/ win solution	• One side resents later • Relationship negatively impacted • Negotiations take time • Collaboration is still possible

APPROACH	SUCCESSFUL WHEN...	POTENTIALLY BACKFIRES WHEN...
Domination	• More important to be right than preserve relationships • Have the authority • Issue is trivial • Emergency	• Used too often • Adverse response anticipated • No attempt to collaborate first

When none of these approaches is used successfully, the team can spiral into a pattern of revenge and self-harm. Individuals may look to win the conflict at all costs, which damage relationships, reputation, and the opportunity to resolve the conflict.

Relationships, personalities, and circumstances may influence which approach works best for a given situation. The shrewd consultant is able to assess the people involved, including their actual versus perceived power, and devise a strategy based on this information. At times, the team may need to shift between approaches to adapt to the opposition. While this may not work in every circumstance, you can follow these basic steps when addressing conflict:

STEP	DESCRIPTION	STATEMENT
1. Confirm	Paraphrase to show understanding	"Yes. I understand that..."
2. Empathize	State the other person's perspective	"I understand why you feel..."
3. Prepare	Pivot from their perspective	"I think we may need to consider..."
4. Provide reasons	Build a case for an alternative perspective	"There are three facts that we need to consider..."
5. Deliver negative statement	Show that you do not agree	"This is why I think we should..."
6. Offer compromise	Provide an alternative solution	"This will enable us to..."

These steps may vary depending on the reactions and approach of a dissenting person or side, what is at stake, and whether the opposition adopts a win/win, win/lose, or lose/lose mentality. For instance, if the opposition takes a lose/lose mentality, there may not be the opportunity to offer a compromise and a leader may need to take on more of a domination approach to reach an outcome. This approach is often used in hostile takeovers, and while not ideal, it is often the only approach available given the personalities, situation, and timeline.

Eric Williamson has led a number of workshops on managing conflict. His strategy: "When dealing with conflict, we tend to let our emotions get the better of us and react without considering the consequences of our actions. This response makes a bad situation worse. Instead of making an impulsive decision when engaged in a heated discussion, we need to take a more measured approach, demonstrate poise, and respond thoughtfully and professionally." Williamson urges us to follow his AAA method: (1) assess the situation, (2) analyze the situation, and (3) act.

BUILDING A CONFLICT-EMBRACING CULTURE

Several strategies can be employed to foster a culture where perspectives are freely shared and people can respectfully disagree. Team-building at the beginning of the project forges connections and enables the project manager to assess personalities. Teammates should seek to build rapport, establish camaraderie, and develop an environment where people are comfortable with each other. Along with that, teams and businesses should begin to design processes before conflict even surfaces so that there is a defined path for addressing it. Establishing processes creates formal paths for conflicts to follow so that expectations can be appropriately managed. Thus, if conflict develops, both the team culture and the processes in place make it easier to get people to share their points of view and respectfully disagree.

As conflict arises, one point to emphasize is that the team is looking for the optimal solution and that this is a business rather than personal issue. Doing so shifts thinking away from personal attacks and toward exploring alternatives. Another way teams can build conflict-embracing cultures is by regularly scheduling "challenge events" where there is open discussion on the status quo and how processes can, and should, evolve over time. Such events highlight the need for change and create opportunities for people to share and explore alternatives. A third approach is recognizing employees who regularly challenge norms by celebrating their ingenuity, providing positive reinforcement, and viewing questions and comments as teachable moments. Finally, setting procedures and ground rules for addressing conflict can prevent team members from drawing disagreement into danger areas. For example, firms may end with a "start doing, continue doing, stop doing" assessment at the end of each meeting or feedback session so that positives along with feedback can be shared.

Conflict can be healthy and provide an opportunity to learn, build better solutions, and grow. Williamson observes that, when managed appropriately,

> Conflict promotes a safe environment that encourages innovative and more creative ways to solve problems and approach different situations. It opens minds and allows people to think outside the box and discover previously unexplored possibilities. This prevents organizations from being stagnant. Instead of doing things because "that's how it's always been done," people will be more open to change and different ways of doing things instead of the same ways people have been accustomed to doing things.

Warning signals should foster discussion that prevents conflict from becoming toxic. Periodic meetings where people can express ideas in a safe environment can be one tool that fosters conflict-embracing cultures. When facilitating these meetings, it is important to ensure everyone participates and that opinions are shared, respected, and valued.

CONFLICT PROVIDES PERSPECTIVE

Eric Williamson's research and experience with conflict shows that it can be devastating to organizations if not managed appropriately. He notes: "People don't leave companies, they leave bad bosses," – or toxic environments littered with unresolved conflict. Replacing these employees can be costly. In fact, it can cost twice as much to replace them than their salary. What's worse than employees leaving? The output from employees who stay! A workplace simmering with unresolved conflict can take its toll, with tensions and frustration often leading to employee disengagement. In fact, according to 2013 Gallup research,[10] 70% of employees are not engaged, and the 18% of employees who are "actively disengaged" can cost the US $450 billion to $550 billion in lost productivity annually."

****

In any work environment, conflict is unavoidable, and in today's increasingly connected world, media distortions, echo chambers, and "fake news" and "alternative facts" facilitate opposition and place the project manager in the difficult position of navigating diverging views. To cope, teams must come equipped with the tools and skills to embrace conflict. While many fear or avoid conflict because they feel that it could damage relationships or take too much time to overcome, many others are learning that conflict can be healthy and should be embraced. Managed well, conflict provides perspective, and addressing it up front may prevent friction from developing to the point where relationships are damaged, ideas for improvement are not shared, and even more time will need to be devoted to meeting demands or rebuilding relationships. Fostering a culture that questions that status quo, is comfortable sharing opinions, and that is curious learning about ideas and perspectives will create a dynamic team that is more able to adapt to the multiple conflicts that inevitably will come. Be ready to embrace it with open arms.

23
HOW DO YOU ADAPT TO VIRTUAL TEAMS?

While virtual teams are nothing new, COVID-19 has forced many companies to adapt and made virtual teams the "new normal." Virtual teams make a lot of sense for many projects – time and productivity may be increased, and costs are decreased, as a result of less travel. No longer constrained by geography, companies also have greater access to larger talent pools. As you launch your consulting career, be prepared to adapt to virtual teams, working across time zones and building relationships with your team and clients in a digital environment.

BENEFITS OF VIRTUAL TEAMS
Many project teams have faced, and are currently facing, the challenges of evolving their projects to a remote environment. The "new normal" of virtual teams opens a host of opportunities while enhancing risks to project milestones, quality, cost, and scope.

In the winter of 2020, our project team faced a tight timeline for a large-scale digital transformation effort. As COVID-19 cases trickled upward across the country, the team had to quickly adapt its onsite instructional training to digital and align the scope of the project with the client and project team remotely. While our quick adjustment to the project created short-term struggles, it did open a number of individual, team, and client benefits. As an individual, I was able to save nearly an hour and a half of frustrating commute time and repurpose it to work on the project, self-care, and spending time with my family. Being home enabled me to take micro-breaks and recharge with smiles and hugs from my five-month-old daughter. Moreover, I was no longer restricted to fitting my job into the traditional workday schedule. The silver lining of being part of a virtual team was more family time, greater comfort, and a more flexible schedule.

While it took some time initially to calibrate, the team was able to align work schedules and a communications cadence and to work productively.

Like me, people could reallocate commute time to the project and other shortchanged activities, and they adjusted their time to meet the needs of the project team. When we had to adjust and tighten project resources on certain areas, the team was able to align hand-offs so that people were able to get up early or work later and finish an aspect of the project before handing it off to other project experts or the client for review.

Being a virtual team also had benefits in regard to talent. Several members of our team were already working remotely before the pandemic hit. This has enabled us to not be bound or limited by geography when hiring. Having a broader radius for talent enabled the team to identify strong performers with the skills needed to drive project results.

With onsite instruction transitioning to digital training, the client was able to save thousands in costs for the nearly 30 people who would have needed to travel for a four-day training. The training was recorded to provide learning artifacts for the client. Moreover, the blended learning model enabled the client to learn at their own pace and allowed them to limit the opportunity costs of their time spent in an on-site instructional training.

RISKS OF VIRTUAL TEAMS

Acclimating to a virtual team environment can open opportunities for flexibility, productivity, and comfort, but it also opens a number of risks and challenges to the project team. As we adjusted to virtual work, we certainly experienced our share of these risks. Digital communication platforms like Zoom are not always the best substitute for a face-to-face conversation. While these platforms do enable you to capture crucial body language features such as tone and facial expressions (a step up from the phone or chat function), project teams do miss out on the more personal touch and added body language of posture. Digital distance can lead to challenges in communicating with the client and within the team and can pose a challenge to relationship building. Moreover, these platforms can sometimes be unreliable when there are a lot of participants in a session. One of our virtual trainings dropped and needed to be restarted because the platform's bandwidth was overtaxed. This led to momentary confusion and loss of flow. Be prepared for Murphy's Law – bandwidth issues will occur at the worst possible moment – and have a plan communicated in case critical virtual meetings do drop.

Morale can certainly be affected. Team members and the client may have fewer costs and more productive time and flexibility, but working remotely also may create heavier burdens. They may not have adequate childcare, may be facing added anxiety and stress over the pandemic, and may miss the emotional recharge of connecting with coworkers at the proverbial water cooler. Calendars can quickly be overloaded with meetings, leading to digital fatigue, and team members can be stuck in a work vortex – forgetting to take breaks for self-care or to recharge. Make sure everyone is building in breaks throughout their day so that they do have time to refresh from screen time. Designate some time to check in with team members to learn how they are adjusting and to connect on a more personal level.

Members of the project may lack immediate resources for remote work. For instance, they may not have the benefits of a home office or even a comfortable working environment. Internet access may be pushed to its limits with multiple people in a household needing to be online for work and educational responsibilities. Distractions can also crop up and pull project members away, causing them to be less productive. Be mindful of these limitations and be aware of what your company can provide to help mitigate some of these issues. For instance, is there money that the company sets aside for setting up a home office? Should there be policies in place to reimburse employees for certain home office–based accommodations?

Accountability can dwindle as it can become more difficult to monitor progress, conduct walk-arounds and check-ins, and maintain a sense of camaraderie. Procrastination or the inability to connect in person can cause hand-offs to slide and project timelines to shift. Moreover, remote teams may face time zone disjunctions. One remote team I'm currently supporting (as of the writing of this book) is working across seven time zones: the majority of the team is operating six hours behind the client, and there is a nine-hour difference between one team member and the client. Time zone considerations require flexibility in planning, adjustments to the workday, and recognition of each team member's location. Setting a common meeting time block can help address these challenges.

As project teams adjust to a digital environment and seek to maintain productivity and effectiveness during a sustained period of remote work, they need to preemptively identify risks and strengthen systems for accountability, communication, and support. Being mindful of the risks of virtual work can lead to better planning and risk mitigation.

LESSONS LEARNED: THREE BEST PRACTICES FOR A VIRTUAL TEAM

To better capture the benefits of a virtual team while limiting the risks, a project team can (1) build culture, (2) establish communications cadence, (3) leverage accountability systems.

1. Build Culture: Showcase Your Personality

Lacking face-to-face communications and the camaraderie of on-site huddles can lead to morale and team culture issues. A virtual culture can be built by taking a servant-leader approach and showing empathy for each project team member's circumstances. Virtual one-on-one coffee breaks with team members can enable you to learn how remote work is impacting them, build rapport, and adapt schedules. Are team members juggling work and watching their kids? Are they struggling with less-than-ideal working conditions? Do they require more flexible working schedules? These conversations can build transparency, deepen trust, and enable the team to better support each other and the client. Just as a project team might conduct a stakeholder analysis and maintain a stakeholder matrix, information from these sessions can be captured and incorporated into broader communications and systems to improve culture and results.

Infuse your personality into your work. Your work environment is now part of your presentation. Set up your workspace to be professional while also showcasing your personality. Your presence now goes beyond just what you are wearing. Invest in a ring light to ensure you look your best – a $20 purchase on Amazon can make all the difference. Make sure you have a professional background that's innocuous with nothing off-putting. A statement piece of art, something that shows your personality or tells a story about you, or a bookcase with some of your most influential books (note – make sure you have actually read these books, in case you are asked about them by your bibliophile client or teammates!) can help provide a clean backdrop and even spark conversation or connection. There have been countless times, while waiting for others to join a meeting, where a book or piece of art caught the client's attention and sparked a dialogue and connection. It's a great way to show your personality!

2. Establish Communications Cadence: Celebrate Personal and Professional Milestones

Regular communications will help strengthen culture and build accountability. Setting regular communications norms such as a daily team huddle or blocked times for work and for meetings can help institute valuable standards. This communications cadence can enable the team to follow scrum principles such as the ability to self-organize, identify, and proactively resolve issues, control and adapt the processes, and be transparent in connecting the dots of their deliverables. This cadence can enable the team to collaborate, prioritize, and set time standards for completing aspects of the project. As part of this cadence, the project team may want to establish certain celebrations or routines. Perhaps on certain days, people appear on video (or appearing on video could be mandatory). Project teams can contribute to culture by having theme days (fun background, favorite hat, show your pet) days. A regular cadence needs to be established with the client to build rapport, manage expectations, and partner to solve challenges. Use it to track progress, recognize contributors, and troubleshoot issues.

Emotional intelligence and "reading the room" are big parts of being consultants. Being on-screen limits your ability to fully read body language. Be extra mindful of your clients' and teammates' tone and facial expressions. In the same vein, make sure you are watching your own tone and adjusting your expressions as the dialogue unfolds. Smile, nod your head, and make hand gestures to emphasize a point. This may take practice and will be something to be mindful of as you work through virtual meetings. Be a good teammate and make culture-building part of your role. Identify opportunities to recognize teammates during meetings, celebrate milestones (personal as well as professional), and share a little about yourself. These gestures help lift the day-to-day doldrums of working through the agenda before the next meeting.

3. Leverage Accountability Systems

Combat procrastination and sliding timelines by utilizing project management tools such as JIRA, Basecamp, Microsoft Teams, or other project management software to set milestones, prioritize resources, and track progress. While establishing a culture of transparency and collaboration and establishing a communications cadence will certainly drive accountability, the project team should document roles, responsibilities, and expectations to guide the team. Project managers should provide the team with a structure and have visibility into what the team and individual members are responsible for. In some circumstances, the project manager may need to establish micro-targets where certain aspects of the project are completed and turned around for review in a short period of time. The project manager may also consider time-boxing tasks to set a firm boundary on when something needs to be completed. When you are on a virtual team, your teammates will appreciate you setting a timeline or time-box, owning a particular aspect of the project, and then delivering within that time frame.

Remote Teams for the Foreseeable Future: The New Normal?

Many companies are seeing the benefits of remote work through cost savings, productivity, and quality of life benefits. Tech giants are instituting long-term policies for remote work, and many companies are considering continuing with remote project teams beyond COVID-19. As remote teams become the "new normal," be sure to make time to build team culture and community, be flexible while also being mindful of individuals' working styles and work-life boundaries, and conduct regular reviews to improve communications and systems. For virtual teams to truly optimize remote work benefits, communication needs to be enhanced to increase trust, transparency, and collaboration. As in any project, communication and continuous improvement are essential. Listening, learning, and implementing feedback up front can help the project manager to better manage time, cost, scope, and quality and lead an overall more effective project.

24

ARE YOU A LIFELONG LEARNER?

As professional problem solvers, consultants thrive in environments where they have to navigate uncertainty and ambiguity, develop a structured way to gather the information they need to efficiently and effectively solve the business challenge, and quickly drive toward a solution. To do this, consultants must be lifelong learners who draw parallels between industries and complex situations, customize and adapt frameworks (and in some cases, build their own), and have a number of go-to resources that they use to build their knowledge and skills across functions and industries.

ATTRIBUTES OF LIFELONG LEARNERS

A March 2016 *Harvard Business Review* article, "Learning to Learn,"[11] by Erika Anderson, summarizes the importance of learning in a world where business models are constantly changing, new technologies are constantly developing, and consumer preferences are constantly shifting. The article cites business theorist Arie de Geus's claim, "The ability to learn faster than your competitors may be the only sustainable competitive advantage." This ability not only represents a competitive advantage for businesses, but also can be a differentiator for the people who form the backbone of these companies. Pushing boundaries, exploring opportunities, and acquiring new capabilities – all while performing your job – enable you to grow and continue to add evolving expertise to your company, community, and clients. The article cites four key learning attributes – (1) aspiration, (2) self-awareness, (3) curiosity, and (4) vulnerability – that enable us to continue to reflect, adapt, and advance on our learning journey.

1. Aspiration: Learning Is an Ongoing Journey

As a change management consultant, I see resistance to change all the time. It is far too common, and indeed, natural for people to focus on the negative aspects of change: *Why do we have to do this? Won't this take too long? Aren't things fine as they are? Don't they realize this will never work?* In contrast, aspirational learners focus first on the positives – how the efforts to learn new knowledge and skills will lead to a brighter future. Flipping the script and focusing on the anticipated long-term benefits and results rather than the short-term losses of time and practice can help drive results. To do this, consultants seek to build awareness and desire to change. We call it the WIIFM – What's in it for me? – and this becomes a critical component of our messaging. Unlocking the WIIFM can be a powerful motivator and a reminder that short-term pain can lead to longer-term gain. Being an aspirational learner can help you overcome initial barriers and build a more agile learning curve.

2. Self-Awareness: Reflecting on Your Gaps

In "Learning to Learn," Anderson writes, "The people who evaluate themselves most accurately start the process inside their own heads: They accept that their perspective is often biased or flawed and then strive for greater objectivity, which leaves them much more open to hearing and acting on others' opinions." Part of ongoing learning is identifying your blind spots and reflecting on your gaps. Being open to continuous improvement and feedback, rather than being defensive, can help you and your team advance.

We sometimes make excuses to protect our ego when we should be digging deeper into the feedback. Feedback is just one person's perspective based on a snapshot, or snapshots in time. Interrogating your own assumptions and perspectives and reverse engineering how people arrived at their feedback for you can help you grow faster. It is worth reflecting on how they reached that perspective and testing that perspective to validate it. Being mindful of feedback can help you spotlight your blind spot(s) and build a plan to address them.

3. Curiosity: Asking the Right Questions

It's been fascinating watching my nearly one-year-old daughter fidget with things, experiment with her toys, and piece concepts together. As we grow older, many of us lose that sense of wonder. People who remain curious ask questions and try something until they can do it or understand it. They find ways to make things more interesting – perhaps tinkering with a process or setting a goal. Curiosity is a language, and constant learners find themselves asking *How? Why? What? Who?* and then actively seek the answers. In consulting, having that sense of curiosity and asking the right questions can often unlock a host of answers. Like a scientist, you observe, you follow a method, form a hypothesis, and sharpen and evaluate – or adjust – that hypothesis as you capture more information. Being able to approach a problem or process with *How? Why? What? Who?* and will help you achieve better outcomes.

4. Vulnerability: Establishing a Growth Mindset

Vulnerability and fear are closely linked, and as we gain expertise and proficiency in other areas, we often become less likely to admit that it takes time to become good at something. Balanced vulnerability is the mindset that you may not be good at something immediately – and that's OK. With practice, you will get better. Psychologist Carol Dweck, famous for her research on the growth mindset, has shown how brain plasticity enables you to grow new connections, strengthen existing ones, and build insulation that speeds transmission of impulses. Brené Brown, whose research on vulnerability should be read by all advancing and aspiring consultants, has written that perfectionism hampers achievement because it leads to analysis paralysis, missed opportunities, and is correlated with addiction, anxiety, and depression. Fear of not meeting expectations keeps us from striving forward and, Brown notes, this self-destructive behavior creates unattainable goals.

There is power in admitting vulnerability. I think I have been at my most authentic self and received the best feedback from my team when I showed vulnerability by admitting that something was not my strength or that I didn't have an answer for a particular situation. Admitting this opens a door for peers – and even more for junior people – to step up, offer feedback, and help you grow. It also enables you to identify strengths on your team and help your team perform at a higher level. When I was vulnerable enough to admit to my team that slides and design were not my strength and that several slides that I had developed might make the team's eyes bleed, they responded good-naturedly and became more open with offering feedback. Several junior members with a keen eye for details even took the lead in updating the slides. While design took me a lot of additional time without the best end result, there were consultants on our team who not only excelled at it, but also considered this work a "fun day." Not only did this admission earn the team's trust, it also enabled several more junior members to step into the limelight and shine, enabled me to learn a few design best practices, and ultimately strengthened the final product for the client. There's no shame in that!

READ!

As a lifelong learner and PPS, you should build ongoing learning into your routines. Whether this is listening to audiobooks or podcasts at the gym, reading on your commute or when traveling, or winding down with a book before bed, learning should become part of your career plan. Since graduating from college, I've made an effort to read an average of a book a week (I've been doing this for nearly 15 years, or nearly 700 books to date!). Most of my reading has centered on business, management, and personal and professional development.

Actively building your knowledge library is a key step to launching your career and growing into a successful consultant. You'll find that books can unify – as you can share favorites and summarize pearls of wisdom with other lifelong learners. Being able to recommend a book or cite findings from a book can help you shape presentations and build credibility.

The "Recommended Reading" section at the end of this book highlights the books that I've found most valuable for consultants at every stage of their careers.

****

The ability to adapt and gain knowledge and skills quickly and continuously will help you advance in consulting (and really, any career). Recognizing that learning is part of an ongoing journey, being aware of your strengths and limitations, asking questions, and being willing to be vulnerable will help you become more than just a good consultant, it'll help you become a lifelong learner.

For further reading, I recommend two books. *Mindset: The New Psychology of Success*[12] by Carol Dweck provides groundbreaking research on how to build a growth mindset. *Grit: The Power of Passion and Perseverance*[13] by Angela Duckworth provides landmark research and insights on how to develop grit to achieve at a higher level.

25

WHICH CERTIFICATIONS SHOULD YOU TARGET FOR CAREER GROWTH?

Certifications are an excellent way to build credibility, advance professionally, and contribute to ongoing learning. A certification can be a distinguishing credential that shows proficiency in certain skills, demonstrates an ability to uphold industry standards, and broadens your professional network. One question that I often get asked is, "Which certifications will help me stand out and advance in my career?" While the trusty answer is "It depends" (on your project, business line, industry, etc.), there are a number of cross-functional certifications that I recommend and that should serve you well no matter your position in consulting: (1) Project Management Professional, (2) Six Sigma (one of the various belts depending on your area of expertise), and (3) Professional Scrum Master.

PROJECT MANAGEMENT PROFESSIONAL (PMP)

The PMP is a foundational certification that will enable you to more effectively contribute to your project team and also prepare to lead a project team. This certification is highly recognized and valued in the industry. It provides tools, templates, and techniques that make you a more effective project manager and opens you to a vast network of professionals and continuing education opportunities. The PMP requires a set number of hours of project management (and you can qualify almost anything as a project), completing 40 hours of training, and passing an exam. To maintain the certification, you will need to complete 60 professional development units/hours (PDUs) over the course of a three-year period. These can include contributing to association and functional knowledge through writing articles, leading workshops, completing webinars and training, attending knowledge sessions, pro bono work, or actual practice of project management principles.

This credential has become almost an expectation for aspiring consultants who look to advance to leading and managing teams, and many clients are making this credential a requirement for any project managers they engage or are willing to pay a premium for project managers who have a PMP.

SIX SIGMA

Six Sigma is a set of tools and techniques centered around process improvement. Often, you will need to help an organization solve a problem by redesigning or simplifying a process. Six Sigma practices improve production and service processes, eliminate defects and waste, and ensure quality. This certification shows you understand factors impacting process improvement. There are various levels (belts): White, Yellow, Green, Black, and Master Black. Each represents progressively greater knowledge, skills, and ability to apply this experience. This certification will be valuable across any industry, and the knowledge can be applied to most projects (fundamentally, most projects will have some element of building or improving processes). It can enable you to reduce project costs, improve productivity, and implement effective processes.

The Six Sigma credential is common across manufacturing but is being increasingly used by consultants. Build your knowledge and understanding, experience, and review the belt that is right for you. Typically, to achieve one of these belts, experience, study, and a test are required.

PROFESSIONAL SCRUM MASTER (PSM)

While more common for Agile projects and IT implementation, a PSM or Certified Scrum Master (CSM), shows that you understand and can apply the Scrum framework for self-organizing teams. (Scrum is a team-based approach to delivering value to the business; it's an empirical process with principles of transparency, inspection, and adaptation.). These certifications focus on professionalizing complex product delivery (typically technology systems). While Scrum may not be used on every project, these principles can benefit teams and help you support the team in aligning skills and efforts.

****

I've made it a practice to obtain a certification every year or so in order to continue to learn and refresh skills, advance professionally, and share knowledge and skills gained from these credentials with my team. Over time, I've obtained over 10 professional certifications (including the three referenced above) and have found that this has enabled me to establish credibility with the clients and project team and apply this knowledge to projects, clients, and industries, making me a much more effective consultant.

Build a plan for earning certifications and work with your manager to identify those that make the most sense for your career goals. Depending on projects and industry, you might prioritize other certifications. Research each one to know the time commitment and cost required to obtain it; what the benefits are; and how it could help you, your project team, company, and clients. While many companies will have a structured way to apply for these certifications, you may need to build a business case to your supervisor on why this certification, why now, and how it will help. Building that business case may also lead to your company supporting you in obtaining it, whether through paying for it or offering you preparation tools – and you may even receive a bonus when that certification is earned.

26

HOW DO YOU OVERCOME IMPOSTER SYNDROME?

Am I really cut out for this? Everyone around me is so accomplished – do I belong here? If I only work harder, will others see that I belong here? Why can't I ever seem to exceed my own expectations? Imposter syndrome is a very real phenomenon that can make insecure overachievers of us all (well, perhaps some people could use a little less confidence and a little more self-reflection). While we may respond in different ways, we do so in ways that are often to our detriment. We strive for positive reinforcement, seek ever greater accolades and achievements to prove our worth, and set Sisyphean tasks for ourselves (and perhaps our teams) to reach a higher bar. All the while, these questions of self-doubt whirl at the expense of valuable headspace for our family and friends, rejuvenation and reflection time for ourselves, and the sanity of those around us.

Imposter syndrome often strikes high achievers, who doubt their accomplishments and have a persistent fear of being exposed as frauds unworthy of their title and achievements, often chalking these successes up to serendipity and "luck." People facing this phenomenon often respond with one of two extremes – overpreparation to more than ensure that they meet that mark or procrastination. When I wrote *Case In Point: Government and Nonprofit* with case interview guru Marc Cosentino, I learned three lessons on how to tame the imposter within.

REFLECT AND REFRAME: HIGHLIGHT YOUR STRENGTHS

When Marc and I began collaborating on *Case In Point: Government and Nonprofit*, imposter syndrome surfaced in full force. I was collaborating with someone who had built consulting and case interviewing expertise over decades, had conducted thousands of case interviews, and who had written *Case In Point* – the best-selling consulting interview "bible" – while I was seemingly just getting started. My mind began to run wild with the countless reasons why someone more experienced, more knowledgeable – more...*not me* – should partner on this book. I had to reflect and reframe.

I had to see that this opportunity was not serendipitous. It came from strengths that I had developed over time. I had to remind myself that *Case In Point: Government and Nonprofit* was a 10-plus-year work in progress that started when I began collecting and developing resources to prepare my younger self for government and nonprofit consulting. It grew when I began sharing these resources as VP of Careers for the Georgetown McDonough School of Business MBA Consulting Club, and it expanded when I began designing and delivering workshops to help students better prepare for the industry.

After graduation, I supported the launch of a public-sector management consulting practice and took ownership of recruiting efforts. With the roles reversed – being on the other side of the interview table – I was able to gain valuable insights into how to identify top-tier candidates. It also gave the chance to track these candidates throughout their careers to see if these qualities correlated to a successful consulting career.

Reflecting on these experiences and reframing to strengths drowned out the incessant questions about needing more experience or not being on the same level of expertise as Marc (and no one is), and also highlighted that I knew the process of preparation more closely than many people – as someone who had been passed up for jobs, as someone who had to deliberate on what distinguished certain candidates, and as someone who made hiring decisions. *Case In Point: Government and Nonprofit* became a letter to my younger self and an opportunity to give others a head start.

TURN TO YOUR PERSONAL BOARD OF ADVISORS

As I've stressed throughout this book, a PBA is one of your most valuable resources and can be a strong reality check for imposter syndrome. These are people who know you, who you trust, and who are not afraid to give it to you straight. They've seen you grow and develop and are invested in your success. I've noted that you may have different PBAs for different aspects of your life and different stages of your career. For instance, I have built a parenting advisory board, general advisory board, and career advisory board. When I began the process for *Case In Point: Government and Nonprofit*, I reached out to my career advisory board, which was composed of mentors, peers, and even people I mentor (again, there is a lot you can learn from your mentees) for advice and to temper the imposter within. Some provided validation, others provided feedback, and others served as readers of the very rough first draft. Through it all, they enabled me to build confidence in the book, strengthen it, and ensure that it remained true to its intent. In true imposter syndrome fashion, I overprepared and ended up cutting probably a full book's worth of content based on their recommendations (second edition out soon?). Your PBA will be a vital resource in quelling that inner imposter, instilling confidence, and generating a stronger product.

WHEN IN DOUBT, HELP OTHERS

There are countless reasons why you should pay it forward and help others. Chances are someone helped you get where you are. Those that you help today may be your helpers tomorrow. More than anything else, it just feels good. It can also help cure your imposter syndrome. Mentoring, coaching, and helping others quiets those inner voices and reminds you of why you are in your position in the first place and that you have valuable insights to share.

When I was drafting *Case In Point: Government and Nonprofit*, I made sure to continue to devote a significant portion of my time to mentoring and coaching others. Students from my undergraduate and graduate alma maters, people from my professional networks, as well as people randomly on LinkedIn, would reach out for advice. Hearing these questions reminded me a lot of my younger self, how much I had learned, and how far I had come. Additionally, it gave me the chance to improve the draft with some real-time coaching and feedback. I walked away from each conversation a little less doubtful, a little more confident, and hopeful that my advice had put them in the position to help others down the road.

****

While we may face imposter syndrome differently, reframing to your strengths rather than focusing on those doubts, relying on a PBA to provide feedback, and helping others can help you treat the imposter within.

27

HOW DO YOU RESPOND TO FEEDBACK?

Being open to feedback and actively implementing it will play a significant role in your career. Establishing that you can listen to feedback constructively, ask clarifying questions, and incorporate it into your practice can help drive your performance and leadership effectiveness. Even a critical or negative message can be valuable, as it can be a warning signal to alert us to gaps and help us more actively monitor our actions. And – *those who seek critical feedback also tend to be better respected by peers and leaders.*

Responding to feedback, particularly negative feedback, is not always easy. First, we have to evaluate our own ego and make sure that we are viewing the situation accurately and without bias. Next, we need to evaluate the source of the message and make sure that the person delivering the feedback is objective, has the right intent, and has an accurate understanding of the situation. Receiving feedback can make us defensive, self-conscious, or frustrated. Ultimately, though, it's an opportunity to improve our effectiveness, so how we respond will affect our ability to implement the critique (positive or negative) and advance.

A great *Harvard Business Review* article, "The Right Way to Respond to Negative Feedback,"[14] provides five tips to manage feedback. Here are how these insights have played out in my career.

TIP 1: DIGEST THE FEEDBACK

Just as you probably are not going to do your best workout on a full stomach, you won't most effectively respond to the feedback immediately. Take a while to digest it. It's also perfectly OK to thank the person who gave the feedback and let them know that you will need to take some time to process it. This will not only prevent you from reacting with anger or frustration, but also will garner respect by showing that you are reflecting on it. Stepping back enables you to take a holistic view and recognize that the feedback does not define you.

Admittedly, this is something that I have needed to work on throughout my career. My initial tactic was to show that I could compartmentalize the feedback and respond appropriately right away to prove that I could manage myself and the critique. This was not always the best approach, especially when feedback was in an email (which is far from the best way to receive it). I've taken to writing email responses on word documents (so they are not accidentally sent) to get my feelings and emotions out and then reviewing and sending a more reasoned reply the next day when possible. I've learned to avoid immediately responding, if I can, since there have been moments where I have reacted defensively by sharing my line of thinking and sometimes disclosed information that the person giving the feedback may not have been privy to. While this may have made me feel like I defended my reasoning, it harmed the relationship and made the person less likely to provide feedback in the future, which ultimately hindered my professional growth. Take time to digest the feedback before responding!

TIP 2: COLLECT INFORMATION

Part of taking time to digest feedback is also taking the time to validate it. Remember that a critique may be based on a snapshot in time or one person's perspective. Build on what you hear by capturing the perspective of other teammates or talking the feedback through with your PBA. Consider things from the perspective of the person giving the feedback. Make sure that you are not falling into the confirmation bias trap by sharing only information that paints your approach positively or seeking opinions only from those whom you know will agree with you. Data can help you sharpen your lens for receiving feedback and also evaluate the messenger.

Often, I would ask my team openly for feedback, and with colleagues, I would give them a scenario and see how they would resolve it. This would not only provide a growth opportunity for the peer, but also enable me to see a different perspective and approach to solving a problem. In turn, I would play devil's advocate and try to ask thought-provoking questions on the approach or talk through the scenario through the persona of different stakeholders and their perceived perceptions.

TIP 3: INDICATE THAT FEEDBACK HAS BEEN RECEIVED

When receiving feedback, find an opportunity to show that you have really listened to it. Sometimes, people who work with us begin to see patterns and ultimately decide that this is "the way you are" and that you "will never change." Show that the message has been internalized and that you are implementing or weighing it.

Once a teammate shared with me that she felt I defended members of the team even when it did not seem warranted. While she did not directly state it, the suggestion was that I played favorites and devoted more time to providing coaching and guidance to some teammates than others. I initially wanted to react defensively and explain that there was more context around those teammates, the project they were working on, and the client that may have warranted sensitivity, empathy, and attention. Instead, I reminded myself that this was an opportunity to listen and learn. I asked clarifying questions and asked for particular examples where she might have perceived me as devoting too much attention, over-defending a teammate, or showing favoritism. These examples enabled me to filter her feedback through my internal lens and compare it with the information I had, as well as recognize that at least one member of the team had this perception – real or not. I thanked her for speaking up and asked her to continue to share examples immediately afterward if she felt I was providing unnecessary coaching or guidance to a teammate or defending someone who she felt was not meeting team expectations. This enabled me to build an ally who could share this perception with me, check myself, and adapt my approach to be more transparent (with the appropriate level of sensitivity) when needed.

TIP 4: EMBRACE FEEDBACK

Research has shown that we tend to avoid people after they have given us negative feedback. If anything, we should show appreciation for their opinion and build a stronger relationship. Through his Stakeholder Centered Coaching approach, leadership expert Marshall Goldsmith tracked the behavior of nearly 11,000 leaders, captured insights, and found that those who engaged in ongoing dialogue after receiving negative feedback showed dramatic improvement. Seeing critical feedback as constructive can help us build the relationship by responding to the person with appreciation, taking their feedback as a learning opportunity, and showing that you value their perspective by implementing their feedback.

Responding well to feedback can turn critics into allies. I found this with a client who was notoriously challenging and who had the reputation of giving harsh feedback to consultants. After repeatedly picking apart presentations, approaches, and meetings (and after I had made efforts to try to avoid this client), I began to engage them more. I took to implementing their feedback and trying to walk through presentations and incorporate their feedback ahead of key meetings. I would share agendas in advance and invite them to propose changes. Paradoxically, the more feedback I sought, the less negative the client's negative feedback became. Eventually, I received the best feedback of all: "You're doing great work. You facilitated a challenging session and were able to keep us moving forward. We accomplished a lot."

TIP 5: ACKNOWLEDGE GROWTH AREAS

We get a higher return focusing on our areas of strengths than trying to shore up our weaknesses. While we can – and certainly should – try to improve our weaknesses, there may be opportunities to compartmentalize. One teammate's strength may be another's growth area. Sometimes acknowledging your weakness and illuminating gaps can be liberating and invite assistance, prompt feedback, and show self-awareness. When I shared that graphics and design were not my strong suit to my team, it opened up the opportunity for support and ongoing feedback. Teammates actually became more willing to share tips and advice to help me grow. Moreover, a more junior teammate who thought of design as a "fun day at the office" and a strength was able to take a more active leadership role. This consultant not only stepped up but enabled me to focus more of my time on my strengths while using their strength in design.

****

Your ability to qualify, respond to, and implement feedback is positively correlated with your career advancement. Build a reputation as someone who is self-aware, actively seeking feedback, and who has a growth mindset pursuing continuous improvement.

Two great books on this topic are *Radical Candor: Be a Kick-Ass Boss Without Losing Your Humanity*[15] by Kim Scott and *The Seven Habits of Highly Effective People*[16] by Stephen Covey.

28

HOW DO YOU ENSURE YOU GET CREDIT FOR YOUR CONTRIBUTIONS?

When numerous people are working on a project with varying levels of visibility, credit can be misattributed or not recognized at all. This can be extremely damaging to morale and can harm team dynamics. Moreover, if team culture descends into credit-seeking behavior, you run the risk of turning your project into a race to claim accomplishments – to the detriment of delivery, productivity, and team trust. A lot more gets done when everyone is not trying to attach their name to everything. Here are three approaches to ensure you get credit for contributions to the project without falling into that trap.

RECOGNIZE OTHERS

Recognizing others for their contributions helps foster a culture of giving credit where it is due. By establishing this type of environment, you build a better team climate and show others that they do not need to fend for themselves for visibility and credit. Make time to particularly recognize those quiet performers whose contributions might be overlooked. This creates goodwill and models a recognition culture. Hopefully, your teammates will return the favor.

OWN SPECIFIC ASPECTS

When you recognize others, make sure that you are highlighting specific actions rather than sharing general praise. This acknowledges the skills and insights that they have brought to the team. As you recognize others' contributions, make sure you are owning the aspects of the project you contributed to. Managers will start to recognize patterns based on what is developed and who owns that piece of the project. Taking responsibility for a particular element of the project links you to the outcome. Make sure that the piece you own contributes to the overall team achievement and helps set the project and team apart.

COMMUNICATE

Be proactive in providing updates to key stakeholders. In most cases, this will be your direct supervisor or project manager. Show that you are in the know by keeping them updated on any key milestones, risks and how you are mitigating them, dependencies, and of course, the contributions of teammates who have gone above and beyond. Project managers and direct supervisors have a lot going on. Being an information conduit that provides them with regular concise, clear updates outlining actions and priorities will help them stay aware of your contributions. Make sure you have identified their preferred communications style and frequency. Will a weekly email update suffice? Should you find time to periodically meet for coffee or informally stop by and share what you are working on? Make sure to balance this communication with their need for information.

****

Getting recognized for individual contributions fosters a collaborative team environment and helps you and your team advance. So give yourself credit where credit is due, and be generous in recognizing others' part in your team's success!

29

HOW DO YOU PREPARE FOR PERFORMANCE EVALUATIONS?

Your performance review is just another way to capture feedback and assess your growth. You should not walk into the room unsure of what is going to be shared or leave surprised by the feedback that you receive. Preparing for a performance review enables you to summarize the goals you accomplished, skills you developed, and impact that you made. Being prepared may not only lead to a better evaluation, but also contribute to promotions, salary increases, or bonuses. While your performance evaluation may occur on an annual basis, your preparation should be yearlong, rather than waiting a few weeks – or even days – before the meeting to summarize your performance highlights.

Shelley Rappaport, who has built her consulting career around performance measurement and evaluation, provided this excellent advice:

> Don't join a firm looking for a roadmap to be partner. The best thing that you can do is focus on growing as much as you can in your current role while looking ahead to the expectations and milestones at the next level. Too often, consultants look several steps ahead without mastering the core skills they need to be successful at their current level. While they may ultimately advance, their career path may be limited as they end up having to course correct or address gaps in their experience later in their career. Too often, people focus on title, and the responsibilities of a particular title will often vary from firm to firm. Title is a guideline, but it is not always the best approach. Focus on the core knowledge and skills that make up your current level and the level directly above and make sure you are able to perform those skills.

Shelley knows – she is currently helping to implement a competency model for her firm that will help guide performance and showcase what knowledge and skills are needed at each stage of that consultant's career.

Here are five steps that I recommend as you prepare for your performance evaluation.

MAP YOUR GOALS TO THE RIGHT LEVEL

As a highly motivated superstar consultant, you should be eyeing the next step in your career and considering what knowledge, skills, and responsibilities you will need to demonstrate at that next level. A partner at my previous firm provided a rough rule of thumb: You should be explicitly showing that you have been operating at the next level for at least six months prior to promotion. This shows that you know what it takes to perform at the next level, are actively performing at that level, and can sustain the effort. As you prepare for your review, you should start by looking at the description, roles, and responsibilities of your current level and the level above. If you are building a case for promotion, make sure that you are taking opportunities and responsibilities to demonstrate that you are performing at the next level. While the position description does not necessarily need to be a checklist, it should serve as a baseline for what you need to accomplish. Exceeding those expectations enables you to build a case for promotion or a higher performance rating. Know these expectations and map your goals to show you are meeting or exceeding these responsibilities.

TRACK PROGRESS BOTH QUANTITATIVELY AND QUALITATIVELY

Both quantitative and qualitative feedback are important when you evaluate your achievements. Tracking your progress qualitatively enables you to build a story and provide needed context around your performance. Qualitative progress may include positive emails from teammates, your manager, or the client. One consultant who reported up to me did a great job maintaining a "wow folder," which included positive comments shared in meetings, emails, and other feedback that demonstrated that they were meeting or exceeding expectations. Being able to reference quotes and emails as part of your evaluation helps you paint a picture of sustained performance, especially if this feedback is being captured throughout the year.

From a quantitative standpoint, this is where you will build on your OKRs and identify the impact you have had. This may include billable hours or utilization rate, proposals you've contributed to and win-rate or total revenue gained from these proposals, professional development hours, or other goals set when developing your OKRs.

One of the things I recommend to my advisees is setting a calendar reminder and making time at least monthly to track your progress. This includes reviewing your goals, reviewing your progress against them, and developing an action plan to address areas where you are not meeting expectations or are falling behind. This also gives you a chance to update your "wow folder" and share key quotes or recognition. Doing this on a regular basis helps you to internalize your goals, be mindful of how your actions are contributing to them, and to celebrate your progress and accomplishments. It also enables you to have more of an ongoing conversation with your manager on your progress and helps you invest your manager in your success and collaborate with them in developing a plan to help you achieve your goals.

BENCHMARK

While I don't recommend comparing yourself to others during your performance review, it can be helpful to benchmark yourself against other high performers at or above your current level in your day-to-day performance. This gives you a baseline model for success and enables you to compare their responsibilities to your own. Moreover, it allows you to evaluate what you are doing and what you should be doing to show that you are performing at a high level. As I've mentioned earlier, the best learning comes from authentic conversations, so when you identify people to emulate, do more than just observe them – share your admiration and actively try to build a relationship. Once you've built that relationship with this teammate, peer, or senior role model, you may want to sit down and have a dialogue with them on what steps and actions they take to achieve high-level performance and what recommendations they have for someone looking to emulate their success. I've been on both sides of these conversations. I've learned a lot from the role models who took the time to meet with me and felt valued and invested in someone's success when they took the time to reach out to me. If you are comfortable, you may even ask them to provide feedback on your performance to date.

COMPLETE A SELF-EVALUATION

While people sometimes get competitive with performance reviews, you are really competing with yourself and should focus on pushing yourself against your own goals. Just as benchmarking provides you with a standard or target to strive for, self-evaluations can help you determine where your gaps are and whether or not you are meeting that standard. Review your position description (or target position description) against your goals and determine how you have adapted, performed, and met or exceeded your goals. Consider the context behind these goals and what qualitative and quantitative metrics you can use to assess your performance. If you have been tracking your progress regularly (monthly), this should be an easy exercise where you are not surprised by your self-evaluation and know where your "Grows" (your gaps and developmental areas) and "Glows" (achievements and strengths) are.

SUMMARIZE YOUR IMPACT

Summarizing your impact can be a balance – you don't want to share every accomplishment, but also don't want to sell yourself short. For each goal, summarize the impact by identifying the most aligned qualitative and quantitative measures. Make sure that your summary is clear and concise and highlights the most important aspects of that goal. Consider whether members of your team or your client might be willing to provide a 360 review of your performance that could be included in your "wow folder" or as part of your impact summary.

In one evaluation, I erred on the side of sharing every accomplishment. My performance summary ballooned to five or six pages, and while the partner of the practice did read every word (or at least he said he did), the feedback I received was that I probably could be more concise. Determine in advance the level of detail your manager is looking for and provide opportunities during regular meetings or informal coffee chats to update them – at that level – on your progress. Summarizing your impact should be a two-way conversation, so it is important to share your honest assessment of your performance as well as highlight key questions or areas where you would like greater feedback.

****

Note that while firms do performance evaluations differently, these steps can help you prepare regardless of format. Some firms may rely more on 360 reviews, others may limit their performance evaluation to a core set of questions – "Would you want to work with this person again?" and "Do you believe this person deserves a bonus (and would you sacrifice your bonus to give it to them)?" Knowing the review process and then continuously tracking your performance can aid you in earning high performance reviews, which can translate into promotions, salary increases, bonuses, and a greater career trajectory.

BUILDING YOUR CAREER

YOUR NEXT 3-5 YEARS

You've run the gauntlet of your early years as a consultant, are earning your stripes, and are beginning to become a grizzled veteran. You've built partnerships, relationships, and alliances and you talk consultant-speak in your sleep. Phrases like "circle back," "20,000-foot view," "boil the ocean," "deliverable," "leverage," and "MECE" are now firmly in your lexicon. You've built solid core knowledge and skills that would be desirable for many industries and other roles. You may even be considering next steps and life after consulting (LAC). As you grind toward those elusive director and partner titles, you may be considering: What steps can I take to differentiate myself? How do I position myself for those next 3–5 years and perform successfully at the next level? Is consulting a viable long-term career option?

During this stage of my career, I asked myself many of these questions and more. As someone who was on the partner track, I evaluated what it took to make partner at my former firm. I took actions to help position myself but also began assessing whether the firm, practice, and career track was right for me. As changes occurred in my personal life, my values shifted, and I also needed to factor this reprioritization into my career plan.

At the time, I was a senior manager feeling the allure of partner while also feeling the squeeze of being upper-middle management. I needed to consider the growth prospects of my practice and team while also considering the growth prospects for me as an individual and how this would affect my long-term career prospects.

There are countless trade-offs and decisions that you will need to make at this stage in your career – most of them centered around how to best advance or whether or not to leave the company or industry. This section will help you to effectively evaluate those decisions and make the career decisions that best positions you for the next level – whatever that may be.

30

HOW DO YOU DIFFERENTIATE YOURSELF?

Setting yourself up for opportunities within the industry and across your firm entails creating pathways to distinguish yourself. At the end of the day, if there are a limited number of promotions or leadership opportunities, or if you are pursuing opportunities elsewhere (or being recruited by headhunters for other opportunities), the person who stands out will have a head start in landing the role they're striving for. Visibility, a strong reputation, and a history of mentoring and coaching others are prerequisites for advancing. There are three additional pillars that can distinguish you from other stellar consultants: (1) initiative leadership, (2) thought leadership, and (3) community involvement.

INITIATIVE LEADERSHIP

Countless opportunities for leading initiatives exist within the cozy confines of your own firm. You can lead an initiative either by developing a business case for a new effort or advancing and taking on increasing responsibility to grow an existing initiative.

Developing a Business Case

If you have come up with a great idea or identified a gap or opportunity, start by building a business case. This can be done by evaluating industry leaders and/or competitors and showing how this idea could differentiate your firm or help it reach parity with these companies, doing analysis of the perceived benefits and costs of the initiative, and perhaps even testing the idea and getting testimonials from a small group of trusted confidants. While each firm may have different processes for evaluating innovations and ideas, pressure testing your idea and building a business case will ultimately strengthen your effort. Establishing a new initiative takes passion, patience, and commitment, and once your idea has run the gauntlet, you'll need to build a coalition of engaged supporters to maintain and grow the effort. During my career, I have initiated, supported, and pressure-tested a range of ideas including (to name a few):

- Corporate social responsibility efforts and prospective pro bono partnerships
- Culture- and team-building efforts and social activities for the practice
- Marketing and business development efforts
- Performance measurement and evaluation and promotion criteria
- Strategic planning and practice OKRs
- Developing the recruiting, structure, coaching, and evaluation of summer graduate interns
- Training and certification program review, requests, and development

Many of these efforts started as grassroots ideas or benchmarking against other firms, followed by building the concept and business case across various levels of the organization. Several started by brainstorming with practice and firm leadership and shaping next steps. Being a founding member of a successful internal project and then growing it from ideation through implementation will enable you to showcase your abilities, build partnerships, raise your profile, and most importantly, help teammates, the practice, and the firm to meet critical goals.

Growing the Impact of an Existing Initiative

Coming up with a great idea and helping the firm implement it is just one avenue. Another is getting involved with an already existing internal effort, being an evangelist for that effort, and enabling that initiative to grow. Being part of a successful initiative creates a halo effect for those actively involved and who are serving in leadership roles. Shaping the initiative, taking on additional responsibilities, and increasing the impact of the effort will help distinguish you in the firm.

****

Many of the ideas raised above spawned opportunities for newly minted consultants and aspiring leaders to take those efforts to the next level. Other areas where I have seen managers successfully distinguish themselves include:

- Building recruiting relationships and partnerships
- Launching or extending an affinity group

• Leading business development proposal efforts

There are a host of internal initiatives already in existence, and many more great opportunities that have not even been developed yet. Consider whether you can commit the time and energy to building out and leading an idea, or whether you will operate better in an already structured existing initiative.

THOUGHT LEADERSHIP

If you are passionate about sharing your learning, growth, and resources with others, then thought leadership is another avenue where you can distinguish yourself. Thought leadership can be packaged internally for the firm, externally for the industry and clients, or modified for both. There are a number of ways that you can showcase – or help you clients showcase – experience, share findings, and better the consulting industry.

- **Brown Bag Lunches:** Internally, you may be able to host brown bag lunches or a learning series where you present on a topic to interested members of your firm. This could be knowledge gained through a project; key takeaways from a certification earned; or tools, frameworks, or best practices that you have used or developed to make you a more effective consultant.
- **Conferences:** Industry conferences or events provide a great opportunity to build a client up by showcasing an innovative solution or a problem that your firm helped solve. It also serves as an opportunity for you to present frameworks, best practices, or takeaways from your experiences. Identifying these conferences and presenting at them helps you extend your firm's brand and elevate your profile and network.
- **Publications:** Author a book or a knowledge article on a business case or topic impacting the industry. While this may be a lot of work (believe me, I know), it can help you reach a broader audience, share and expand your ideas, and more broadly establish your expertise.
- **Training:** Design training, modify an existing training course, and deliver this training to colleagues and up-and-coming consultants. This provides another opportunity for you to showcase your knowledge, experience, and skills and have a multiplier effect in your firm by helping others to use these lessons learned. Being recognized as a firm expert can help you enhance your reputation and contributions to the firm.
- **White Papers:** Many firms publish white papers as a way to demonstrate expertise, share findings, and potentially build business. Prospective clients are often comforted by knowing that a firm has successfully solved a similar business problem before. Industry

professionals and aspiring consultants alike may learn and gain from these white papers, and authoring them can help establish you as a knowledgeable resource both internally to the firm and externally to the industry.

Different firms look at thought leadership differently and may have particular structures to govern it. For instance, some firms require a lengthy review and approval process before anything goes public or references a client, project, or employee. Others have built thought leadership apparatuses that actively seek and promote the work of their consultants. Still others are decentralized and enable you to craft thought leadership independent of the firm. Learn your firm's practices around thought leadership and determine which option is best.

COMMUNITY INVOLVEMENT

There are many ways to get involved in your community, and tying these experiences to your firm's brand and the skills and network you develop will help you differentiate and distinguish yourself in not only your community, but also your firm. While community involvement is a best practice we all follow, make sure you get credit for it in the professional realm as well. Share your community involvement with your manager and build this involvement into your career plans and goals. Highlight the benefits that you are gaining from this experience and see if there are ways to align your firm initiatives with your community experience (is there an opportunity for a partnership, volunteer or pro bono work, corporate social responsibility, or way to market and profile your involvement?).

One particular aspect of community involvement is to join the board of a nonprofit. This is not only rewarding in itself, but also an invaluable experience for career growth and development. As a longstanding member of three boards (serving as chair/president of two), I've seen how board service can strengthen your community while also helping you put your time and talents to good (better?) use. In joining a board, I've been able to learn from the perspectives of people from different backgrounds, generations, and professions; build a stronger network; and collaborate to solve complex challenges.

When I posed the question of community involvement to Yashomati Bachul Koul, they shared the importance of dedicating time to things that you are passionate about. Koul serves on the board of LYRIC, a nonprofit that "envisions a diverse society where LGBTQQ youth are embraced for who they are and encouraged to be who they want to be." Koul, who identifies as trans/non-binary, was committed to finding a way to take their consulting skillset and find a way to give back to their community. Koul is able to bring their organizational leadership and board governance experience to the work they do as a board member for LYRIC. Koul is also engaged in several initiatives around diversity, equity, and inclusion (DEI) at Kearney. Koul advises,

> It is par for the course that when you first join your firm, everything sounds exciting and you want to sign up for every firm building opportunity. You sign up to participate in recruiting, and support business development, and write articles and very soon, your calendar is oversubscribed and what had started as joy/excitement is now dread/exhaustion. You need to check yourself and focus on what you are passionate about. When I look back, the people who have unlocked the code to a successful career path the fastest have been the ones who took control of their careers from day 1. This means they not only had a plan, but they never ceded control over their careers to internal process or expected timelines. They did this by having a clearly defined platform – one that they were passionate about and that enabled them to weave project work, practice alignment, business development, idea creation, etc., into a cohesive narrative that clearly identified and differentiated them as experts in the space they defined for themselves.

****

While you are undoubtedly giving back to an organization because you are passionate about their cause, believe in paying it forward, and want to serve your community, there are also professional benefits to joining a nonprofit board. It creates camaraderie, extends your network, and helps you to develop and apply skills in new and distinct ways as you solve problems and lead in another context. Board service can be valuable at any stage of your career (and for those earlier in their careers, many nonprofits have "advisory boards" or regular volunteer groups that could be a stepping-stone to a board seat). Leverage your network and skills for good and enrich your life, as well as the lives of others impacted by the cause, by joining a nonprofit board!

31
HOW DO YOU BUILD YOUR INFLUENCE?

Your network, who you mentor, and who mentors you should be very intentional decisions that can help you expand your sphere of influence. When your associates and mentees succeed, you benefit from some of that halo effect, but tread lightly and mentor wisely because failures can also reflect on mentors. Visible leaders can help elevate your status and your rising star disciples can extend your network and open you to building relationships with other colleagues and high performers in their orbit. In today's business world, informal power and influence are becoming increasingly pivotal to your impact and success and can contribute to more formalized influence as you ascend the corporate ladder. While your formal title and direct reports can contribute to your influence, this pales in comparison to your reputation and the informal relationships that you have built across the organization.

The *Harvard Business Review* article "How to Figure Out How Much Influence You Have at Work"[17] recommends conducting a "power audit" to identify where your influence resides and where you have gaps. The article advises that you:

1. List the top 10 contacts who enable you to complete work.

2. Assign a score of 1–10 for each contact, with 1 being no dependence on that contact and 10 if that contact is essential to you completing work.

3. Attempt to do the same in reverse by assigning yourself a score based on what you perceive that contact's perspective to be. Be honest and humble in considering how (in)dispensable you are to that person's success.

When conducting your power audit and attempting to build your influence, consider (1) organizational structure, (2) asymmetries in the relationship, and (3) concentration.

ORGANIZATIONAL STRUCTURE

Where does your influence reside? Is it distributed in one group or spread across areas of the firm? Building relationships is an essential element of succeeding in consulting. Take time to get to know people beyond your project team and practice and across levels of the firm. The more widely distributed your network is, the more people you have to tap into for skills, knowledge, and connections.

ASYMMETRIES IN THE RELATIONSHIP

Who is providing the value in the relationship? Relationship asymmetries can show dependence. If you are dependent on the majority of your contacts, then this overreliance can lead to more temporary or transactional relationships. It may also limit your power and ability to influence these contacts. On the flip side, if your contacts are overly reliant on you, then you run the risk of reaching a plateau in your influence. Ideally, your relationships will be a mix where you provide a mentoring or manager relationship to acolytes growing their careers; mutually support peers and colleagues; and have more seasoned benefactors providing mentoring, coaching, and advocacy for your career.

CONCENTRATION

Is your influence based solely on a few contacts? Diversifying your power dynamics and distributing your influence across contacts enables you to not be fully dependent on one group. For example, one consultant had built strong relationships with her project team and client, but her firm failed to recognize the disproportionate power dynamic that had developed. When she was laid off during the COVID-19 downturn and a more junior staffer was placed on the project, the firm ended up not only losing her but also losing the client! Because of this consultant's strong ties to and influence with the client, the client felt more loyalty to her than they did the firm and ultimately reached out to her to see if she would serve as an independent consultant for them. Had the firm diversified relationships and put eggs in more than one basket by rotating consultants or enabling other consultants to build relationships with the client, they might have ultimately retained this client by having more distributed relationships to leverage.

****

Recognize that your value is not based solely on your formal role. Influence can be manufactured, and once you identify your gaps, you can build a strategy to help you extend it. Identify opportunities to realign asymmetric value relationships with your contacts. If you are providing less value to the relationship than your contact, see if there are ways that you can take on more responsibility, provide additional support, or be an advocate for that contact. On the flip side, if you are the one providing more value, see if you can coach them or create pathways for them to contribute more to your career growth as you help them advance. One question that I always ask contacts – both those I report up to and those I oversee is "What can I do to support you and help you to be more successful?" Take careful note of how they respond.

Make yourself indispensable by contributing beyond your formal job description. Go beyond the traditional role by taking part in cross-functional firm initiatives and placing yourself at the crossroads of key intersections in the firm. Participating in and contributing to a number of different initiatives may help you extend your relationships and contacts and also add more value to those contacts. But as with anything, prioritize your commitments and focus on quality over quantity. Overextending yourself can weaken your networks, since you won't have time to nurture the relationships that really matter.

A key component to building relationships is getting to know people outside of day-to-day work. Learn about your coworkers and teammates on a more personal level. Knowing their kids' names, celebrating their life milestones, or being more aware of their personal situations can help you tailor your contributions and build goodwill for when you do need some help.

****

The more you advance, the more formal clout you obtain. However, don't lose sight of the informal influence that you earn and establish beyond just your job title or role. This will help you manage and overcome politics; build coalitions; and tap into knowledge, networks, and expertise that can extend your capabilities and influence.

32

WHY SHOULD YOU FOCUS ON YOUR "B" PLAYERS?

No firm will be composed only of all-stars. Nor should they be. Many firms undervalue their solid, reliable "B" players, who may have different motivations and worldviews and are contributing at different levels than your typical "A" all-stars. Discounting "B" players is a huge mistake that many teams often make – to the detriment of client and team relationships, firm dynamics, and retention. Defining individuals' strengths and capabilities, knowing their motivations, and knowing the drawbacks of each teammate can help you build your team, strengthen your influence, and increase productivity.

WHAT IS THE DISTINCTION BETWEEN "A," "B," AND "C" PLAYERS

A typical organization may be made up of 10% all-star "A" players, 80% dependable "B" players, and 10% mediocre "C" players (these are not the same as poor performers; hopefully, you have eliminated those!).

"A" players have been recognized for their high potential. They are promoted faster, given more opportunities to contribute, and are resourceful, effective, and high-performing leaders. They bring energy, passion, and adaptability to the team and are often recognized and rewarded for their performance. "A" players tend to attract other "A" players or can help propel "B" players to becoming all-stars. On the flip side, these "A" players have their downsides. They are more likely to take risks, have their ambition cloud their judgment, and seek accolades, promotions, and leadership at the expense of their teammates. Moreover, their aspirations for the next level make them more prone to being flight risks or becoming competitive with other "A" players vying for alpha status.

"B" players are solid performers. They are often the bulk of your workforce, have good skills, and are competent, steady performers. These teammates are often comfortable in their role, have built relationships over their tenure with the firm (and often they tend to stay put), and are able to share institutional knowledge, connections, and corporate history with the team. They are the glue that can keep the team together. While ambitious, they may be more willing to make sacrifices for the good of the team or company.

"C" players tend to be performing at or below expectations. They do the bare minimum, but enough to fly under the radar. They tend to stay until they are fired or held accountable. "C" players may have started as "B" players but lost motivation or engagement with the firm.

The late management guru and former CEO of General Electric, Jack Welch, famously advocated promoting and providing greater opportunities for "A" players to thrive, retaining and developing "B" players, and neutralizing or firing "C" players. But companies approach performance management differently. I've seen the gamut – from companies with a stringent "up-or-out" culture to others that are more flexible in coaching to others tolerating mediocre performance as long as that consultant is generating revenue.

WHY "B" PLAYERS MATTER

The *Harvard Business Review* article "Let's Hear It for Our 'B' Players"[18] provides powerful insight into the importance of these teammates. While you can aspire to build a team of "A" players, "B" players are dependable team players who often quietly and consistently get the job done. While "A" players may be looking for that next career-advancing move, "B" players' modest ambitions can help moderate the often-fraught dynamics between attention- and credit-seeking "A" players. While "B" players do seek rapid advancement, they focus on work-life balance and relationships, and are often barometers for the company. They may play the role of "truth-tellers" who provide honest responses to questions around the team and company dynamics. As "B" players tend to stay in one place, they often are the company's historians and go-to people for helping others navigate the firm and its people and processes. Many feel a loyalty toward the company for giving them an opportunity, helping them grow, and letting them advance at a steady pace.

The stability "B" players provide can be indispensable. They may not necessarily bring in the business of the "go-big or go-home" "A" players, but their consistent performance can help limit risks. Because "B" players are considered reliable, trustworthy, and balanced, they play an important role during transitions or management changes. This affords them a critical role as dependable observers who artfully avoid the political fray and truthfully share their perspective on the state of the firm. This role fosters credibility and their own influence within the firm.

Like any teammate, "B" players need attention, encouragement, and appreciation. Managers need to recognize that not everyone shares their perspective or worldview (and may not be aspiring to be a rockstar like themselves). While "B" players may not actively seek time or accolades, that does not mean that they do not deserve time and respect. Managers should regularly meet with "B" players for reliable feedback and to get a pulse on the team, as well as to see how they can best support their career growth and contributions to the team. They should provide "B" players with choices that help them manage their careers and contributions and should regularly recognize them for their contributions. This will not only aid retention and the overall productivity of the team, but it also will help build your influence and credibility with a vital population of the firm. Do not overlook these essential members of your team!

I recommended a hire who was deemed to be an atypical consulting candidate. This person came from a nontraditional background and was not your conventional confident and charismatic candidate in the interview. I assured the company that his unassuming style would be great for building relationships, that he was a team player who sought to lift others up and bring people together, and was eager to learn, grow, and contribute. While he lacked many of the "standard" consulting qualities, he had many overlooked attributes that would make him a strong addition to the firm. Too often consulting firms and project teams limit themselves and miss out on great hires by seeking to hire those who think like themselves or fit their paradigm of a consultant. While the interviewers were looking for charisma, confidence, and "executive presence," they missed the "hustle factor," authenticity, and willingness to learn that this consultant displayed. This consultant was an exemplary "B" player, steadily advancing, consistently learning and putting himself in positions to learn and grow, and adapting to the needs of the client and the firm. He took the less-than-glamorous assignments, ground through projects outside of his comfort zone, and sought ways to glue the team together. He did not push for a fast-track promotion and was loved by the client to the point that they tried to hire him for an in-house role. Several "A" players shone like supernovas before extinguishing or succumbing to the gravitational pull of ambition to other projects or firms. The project team valued this "B" player's consistency and the relationships that he had built over time and considered him critical to their winning a multimillion-dollar contract.

****

Not everyone needs to be an "A" player – and organizations and their leadership need to see value in different perspectives and mindsets. Firms are a mosaic, and recognizing the contributions that all consultants bring will increase your influence and ability to lead. Most importantly, this acknowledgment will help you build more effective teams and attract, engage, and retain a crucial element of your organization.

33
HOW DO YOU MANAGE UP?

Communication and emotional intelligence are major aspects of your role as a consultant. As you advance in your career, you'll find that you are defined less by your technical skills and more by your ability to manage conflict, build relationships, and communicate opportunities and results. Your ability to "manage up" can shape your career more than any of those other skills and talents.

These six strategies are invaluable for managing up.

DEFINE YOUR BOSS'S STYLE

A big part of managing up is being able to understand and adapt to your boss's leadership, communication, and decision-making style. Sometimes explicitly asking your boss for their preferences around communication can help you build awareness and show that you value their time. When you get an answer, make sure to listen and then implement this feedback in your interactions. For instance, your boss may have set hours where they respond to work or prefer to communicate. They may be better reached by email, phone, or text. They may prefer to be updated periodically or only contacted when something needs to be escalated for their review or a decision. Setting these guidelines up front and then adhering to them can help you build a relationship and strengthen your connection with your boss.

When you do get those precious moments of your boss's time, consider what information works best for them. Do they prefer that you send something ahead of time so that they can review and digest it before responding? Do they respond better to stories, facts and data, benchmarks and research, outlining the risks? Do they prefer you to come with a solution to a problem (which you should always have in place) and share your approach or do they prefer to work through the problem with you?

If your boss does not share their communication style with you, watch how they interact with others or see if you can learn from others who have worked with this boss before. Develop guidelines with your boss on how they prefer to receive updates and what items should be escalated. Part of defining your boss's style is also defining your own approach. If the way you frame your communication clashes with your boss's, adapt your approach to better meet their needs.

UNDERSTAND THEIR GOALS

Part of your goals should be to make your boss look good. Knowing what motivates them and what they are measured on can help in two ways: (1) it gives you something to strive for when you someday reach that role, and (2) it helps you build goals that cascade up into supporting your boss's performance. Whether it is retaining or building business with a client, developing the project team, or helping them raise visibility of the project or advance a particular initiative, your success is intertwined with your boss's success. Recognize that you are part of the same team and that the more you can collaborate on helping your boss achieve their goals, the more they will recognize you for your performance.

ANTICIPATE THEIR NEEDS

Knowing your boss's styles and goals can help you to better anticipate their needs. Being able to think through the next steps (or five next steps) and share that you have thought through various approaches, are considering the information they need, and know how these steps will align with their goals will help you manage up. Just as a good teammate anticipates the needs of others on the team, a good consultant can also show their boss that they can be trusted in thinking through the next steps. Take a holistic approach to your project and recognize that there are many stakeholders with many (hopefully aligned) needs. Show your boss that you are thinking through where potential shortfalls and blind spots are and have developed an approach to address them.

SHARE STRATEGIES TO UTILIZE YOU

Demonstrate that you are self-aware of your strengths and gaps and share approaches with your boss on how he or she can more effectively utilize you or other members of the team. This not only allows you to shine by showcasing your strengths, but also enables you to highlight ways that the team can operate more effectively. Come to your boss with well-thought-out ideas and talk through your plan with them. Make sure they are aware that these observations are based on your understanding of yourself or experience working with the team and that you are partnering with your boss to see how these ideas can be made more effective.

HONOR THEIR TIME

Time with your boss is precious, and each interaction is an opportunity to make an impression. Show that you value their time by coming with a plan and bringing opportunities and solutions rather than problems. Recognize that they have many competing priorities. Provide information to your boss in advance whenever possible, so that they are not blindsided. Walk through context with them quickly and make sure that your interactions are clear, concise, and have an objective in mind. This shows that you are valuing your boss's time – and let them take your conversation into another direction if they desire.

BUILD RAPPORT AND EMPATHIZE

Valuing their time and building rapport can sometimes be seemingly competing interests. Find that balance. Work in personal tidbits about you and your experience during your conversations and see if this opens the door to sharing personal information that helps build a stronger professional relationship. Knowing what is going on in our boss's life can help you adapt your style and approach to their situation. Moreover, it helps you build and demonstrate empathy and awareness.

****

Helen Walker is a teammate of mine who I have seen artfully manage up, across, and in every which way. For over 15 years, she has managed digital transformation efforts, led training, and overseen international teams. I've seen Helen use exceptional emotional intelligence skills to build relationships across client and project teams. When I asked her to define managing up, she shared that it really came down to two elements: "One is helping to instill confidence so that the manager can focus time and attention elsewhere while you adapt to your lane. The second piece is determining where you can use your unique skills to fill gaps or take on responsibilities that enable your manager to be more effective and successful. When they succeed, you succeed."

In her experience, Helen shared, all management is about

...establishing relationships, showing respect, and providing the right level of attention. Whether managing down, up, or across – it is figuring out where you fit and how you can help that person to grow and be successful. When you manage up, it is with curiosity and respect. You want to do research to better understand why an approach is being taken or how your approach would work. Take a fact-based approach so that you are best utilizing your manager's time and providing them with approaches that are grounded in facts.

Helen highlighted an essential part of managing up – humility: "A huge skill that is underestimated in 'managing up' is humility. Part of this is determining where they are at, respecting where they have been, and determining how you fit into supporting them." That being said, managing up also takes balance, which is part of what makes it so challenging. Helen further noted, "I feel many people put their managers on a pedestal and feel like they need their manager's approval for everything rather than taking the initiative or taking the lead on an effort. Don't be intimidated by the position or title, take an approach that this person is human, trying to advance in their career, and your role is to help them."

****

When in doubt, ask your boss, "How can I help make your life easier?" Do not be surprised if they are initially taken aback by this, as they are used to putting out small and large fires all day. Knowing that they have someone in their corner looking to help them direct the hose to the fire or even operate the hose for them to put out the fire can go a long way in your relationship.

34

HOW DO YOU MENTOR OTHERS?

Paying it forward and contributing to ongoing learning are part of being a strong leader and successful consultant. Positioning others for success can have a multiplier effect by increasing the effectiveness of your team, creating a leadership pipeline, and enabling you to grow your network and influence. Being a mentor enables you to build patience and coaching skills, become a better leader, gain fresh ideas and perspectives, and adapt communications styles and approaches to a different generation or group. It also provides you with the opportunity to reinforce lessons you've learned (and maybe serve as a refresher for yourself) and to shape the perspective of future leaders. Mentoring takes time and commitment, but prioritizing this aspect of your career can lead to individual (your own and your mentee's), team, and firm growth.

BE A TRUSTED ADVISOR

Mentoring and coaching is about being a trusted advisor. This can happen at distinct levels of the organization – with peers, with junior staff, and even with more senior staff. Being a mentor goes beyond a professional relationship, as you can provide life coaching and advice that could also shape personal decisions. To be an excellent mentor, you need to customize and tailor your approach to the individual. They may need mentoring on a specific aspect of their career or for a particular phase. Establish expectations and determine what a successful mentorship would look like. This is something that should be done collaboratively and requires the trust on both sides. Mentoring is a partnership, and you both need to be committed and hold each other accountable.

BE INVESTED IN YOUR MENTEE'S SUCCESS

Mentorship is about more than time or WIIFM (what's in it for me?). To be a great mentor, you need to be truly invested in that mentee's success. Hold yourself accountable in helping that person achieve their goals and also hold them accountable by guiding and coaching them. Part of becoming invested in the mentee's success is getting to know them personally as well as professionally. Learn more about their values, what matters to them, and who they are as a person. This helps you become a more trusted advisor and will forge stronger bonds that make you more devoted to their success.

BE AN ACTIVE LISTENER

Part of being a mentor is being a good listener. I often advise people to apply the "80/20" rule to mentorship – the mentee does 80% of the talking. Spend more time listening than advising, and distinguish between when your advice and opinion are sought and when your mentee just needs to share something. Other times, you play Socrates and use the dialectic question-and-answer approach to guide them to a resolution. Just as in consulting, a carefully crafted question can unlock a door to a tremendous wealth of information. Becoming carefully attuned to your mentee's body language and leveraging those strong emotional intelligence skills that you have undoubtedly developed at this stage will help you play a stronger role. Learn when to hit the "pause button" and take a break to allow you both to digest any information and let your mentee direct the next steps.

SHARE LESSONS LEARNED

Part of the reason I'm writing this book is because I get a lot of the same questions about consulting, have many conversations on these topics, and want to share some of the hard lessons learned so that others don't repeat my mistakes. Part of being a mentor is about being forthcoming about mistakes you've made and sharing how they've shaped your career. Be mindful, however, that this is a learning experience for your mentee, and that your advice, feedback, and guidance is just one piece of the puzzle that may shape their ultimate approach.

CELEBRATE THEIR ACHIEVEMENTS

Being a mentor is about helping your mentee develop a roadmap for success. Share resources, courses, or initiatives that can help them build the knowledge, skills, and network to advance. When they succeed, recognize and acknowledge progress and celebrate these accomplishments. This reinforces your messaging, models positive mentorship that they can emulate when they themselves are in a mentoring role, and keeps them motivated and invested in the relationship. Your support can also have a trickle-down effect for the more junior personnel that your own mentees will eventually mentor. Moreover, celebrating successes balances out some of those more feedback-oriented sessions that you will inevitably have.

SET THE EXAMPLE

Mentorship is paying it forward so that others can benefit from your time and experience. Your mentees are your disciples, and they are not just looking for you for guidance, but also to you as a paradigm for their future self. They will be observing how you behave inside and outside of your meetings and will emulate you. Acknowledge when you've made a mistake or did not set the right example and strive for giving them the best example to live by.

I'm proud to call Dave Brant my mentor. One of the world's foremost experts in counterterrorism, a public servant employed in the Naval Criminal Investigative Service (NCIS) for nearly 30 years (including serving as director from 1997 to 2005), Dave has had an illustrious career. After retiring from government, Dave held leadership roles at Deloitte, launched BDO's public-sector consulting practice, and served as a museum executive. He's a consummate professional who considers mentoring future leaders a duty and who has provided me with insights that have shaped my career.

When I asked Dave about what it takes to be a great mentor and what to look for in a mentee, he said both should have similar attributes – just apply them differently. He summed this up as, "Listen. Learn. Act. Active listening requires capturing information and building on what you know by asking the right questions. Learn from the perspective and what was shared. There is a responsibility on both the mentor and mentee to act. The 'act' part is extremely important and can be applied to a number of scenarios beyond mentorship." Dave has found that the people who make the best mentors and mentees are able to listen to another's perspective, understand and learn a bit more about that person's history and what shaped that perspective, and ask questions that unlock greater information.

****

Being a mentor is an honor and a recognition that you have valuable experience and insights to give. It shows that someone is aspiring to be more like you. Take this opportunity and build a following that can help you, your team, and firm advance.

35

HOW DO YOU GIVE FEEDBACK?

Giving feedback, especially around opportunities for improvement, can be challenging. Many very adept consultants and managers avoid it because they do not want to hurt someone's feelings or alter team dynamics. Giving feedback can be uncomfortable, both for the recipient and the one doling it out. Few managers do this well – to the detriment of the team. Poor feedback can lower morale, productivity, and team performance. It can limit your teammates' ability to improve, excel, and achieve, which, as a team leader, can hinder your own abilities. The fundamental driver of feedback should be about how we enable that person to thrive and excel in their role. Feedback is about (1) learning and growth, (2) empathy, (3) actions, and (4) prioritizing excellence. These four feedback "musts" will enable your team to take a LEAP in their ability to achieve.

LEARNING AND GROWTH

Fostering a love of learning and growth in your team comes with making feedback about the journey rather than about what they are doing wrong. Giving feedback based on failure and providing tips on how to avoid it seldom leads individuals to the opportunity to experience failure, learn from it, and achieve. When giving feedback, focus less on how to do something differently and have more of a conversation. Ask open-ended questions: What did that person observe? Why did they choose a particular method? What would they have changed? What did they gain from the experience? The dialectic method inspires reflection and makes feedback a two-way conversation rather than a passive, one-sided perspective on what the manager observed and how the person receiving the feedback could have done it better. Build learning and growth habits and make these questions part of the process. This will enable your team to take ownership of their learning and growth and focus on what they can do better rather than what they did wrong. When you focus only on what went wrong, it is hard to fortify and build on what went right!

EMPATHY

Feedback works best when you have built a relationship of empathy and support. Placing yourself in the mindset of the person receiving the feedback and being open with your reactions, feelings, and emotions enables you to build a culture of trust and even vulnerability with them. It is in vulnerability that we experience growth and are willing to be open and candid, and to challenge our egos. Empathy can be established and modeled by sharing personal anecdotes where you learned from mistakes, expressing your gut reactions so that your authentic self is on full display, and also openly sharing your emotions and even naming the emotions that your teammate may be feeling – pride, frustration, anxiety, satisfaction, etc. Empathy creates an atmosphere of care and the conditions for that person to excel because they know you are with them in the trenches, working alongside them, and sharing with them what they are doing to excel.

ACTIONS

The *Harvard Business Review* article "The Feedback Fallacy"[19] emphasizes the importance of actions that produce outcomes. It showcases the powerful, outcome-based approach that legendary Dallas Cowboys football coach Tom Landry used for his team. Rather than combing through game films for mistakes, Landry created highlight reels of players performing actions that led to successful outcomes. The team would review these films to learn what they did effectively in that instance and then dissect these actions. This positive reinforcement emphasized excellence rather than remediation. This praise approach provided individuals and the team with successful patterns that they could review, reform, and refine to lead to greater success.

PRIORITIZE EXCELLENCE

Feedback works best when it is specific and frequent. Just as Tom Landry did with the highlight reel, when you see someone on your team performing well in the moment (during a prep session, whiteboard session, or immediately after a client meeting), elevate giving feedback for this in your queue of things to do. Stop the session when possible and dissect in the moment what that person is doing and why it is so effective. Invite the team to share their responses and provide praise and feedback as well. At first, this can be awkward, but it serves three primary purposes: (1) it recognizes and rewards excellence in the moment, (2) it provides a model for teammates to emulate, and (3) it involves the team in the feedback process, creating a culture of learning and growth. Recognizing specific instances of excellence and prioritizing these actions in the moment enables the team to dissect and digest the action. This builds a roadmap toward excellence that others can follow.

****

How to give feedback was one of the hard lessons I learned through countless mistakes and moments when I reflected on why my message was not being received and what I could do to deliver it more effectively. As a team leader, your ability to give feedback is inversely related to your stress around it; being able to successfully distill feedback and work through challenges will lead to less stress. The more you shy away from giving feedback or the less effective you are at doing it, the more mistakes and issues will arise and repeat themselves.

When a relatively new consultant joined my team with well-aligned prior experience and an MBA, I was ready for that consultant to take off and run with their piece of the project. A few issues started to arise as crucial details were missed, presentations lacked the needed specificity, and the client started losing confidence in this consultant. When I offered feedback, the consultant responded first with frustration, then got defensive, then redirected her frustration at the client and my ability to give feedback. We were at a crossroads – she seemed exasperated enough to quit, which would severely hamper the project. I wondered if we had missed critical details in hiring.

When I peeled the onion further, I looked inward into the coaching I was providing and found the turning point. I uncovered that the feedback I was giving her was more one-directional and focused on what needed to be changed rather than on what was going well. I needed to reset our relationship, and that started by acknowledging that this was a shared learning experience and journey for both of us. It also required building a relationship based on empathy and adding a more personal touch. Part of this came with sharing the emotions that I was feeling and knew that she was probably feeling in the moment, sharing that I had similar experiences and shortcomings, and that growth came from these frustrations. Once we had established an emphasis on growth, our relationship shifted from more of a manager-consultant relationship where the consultant felt judged to a mentor-mentee rapport where the consultant felt like I was coaching her to excel. She became more comfortable in proactively coming to me to talk through potential issues and approaches, share her thought processes, and work through actions we could take to improve outcomes. My approach shifted from corrective action to enabling and supporting actions. This consultant went from nearly quitting – which would have harmed relationships with the client, stretched our team, and dimmed the halo of my hiring history – to strengthening her ties to an executive client and building out a new area of business.

****

There are myriad cutting-edge as well as tried-and-true methods to giving feedback and at the end of it all, you may need to adapt your approach to the individual, team, and culture of your company. Whether it's the "radical transparency" model employed by financial juggernaut Bridgewater Associates – where 360s occur on the spot, all meetings are recorded and reviewed later, and employees have public "baseball cards" with their performance statistics – or the oft-used feedback sandwich, providing timely, specific, and empathetic feedback can increase individual and team performance. Employing a learning and growth mindset, showcasing empathy, focusing on effective actions that led to successful outcomes, and prioritizing excellence will help you build a successful team and take a LEAP in your career.

Undoubtedly, you'll need to adjust and adapt your own approach to fit the culture of your team and company. I recommend reading *Radical Candor: Be a Kick-Ass Boss Without Losing Your Humanity*[20] by Kim Scott to discover best practices on creating a culture of feedback, collaboration, and achievement.

36

HOW DO YOU BUILD LASTING CLIENT RELATIONSHIPS?

"Consultant" can be a dirty word for a lot of clients. For many organizations, consultants are viewed as paid hire, mercenaries, and a reminder that the organization lacks the internal know-how to get the job done. Critics snidely remark that "consultants borrow your watch to tell you the time, then forget to give it back (and charge you for it)." Walking into this minefield can be a challenge, and while many consultants are respected and held in high esteem, they must first build credibility and trust before they can provide advisory support. Trust is the key to building lasting client relationships – and lasting client relationships are the ladder to longevity in consulting.

Trust is built by being reliable, consistent, and showing integrity. This is established by avoiding water-cooler gossip, recognizing that your role is to advise and not to dictate (in the end, it is the client's decision), being a thought partner who works through challenges collaboratively and thinks through the options and alternatives, and providing reasoning to support your assumptions and conclusions. Trust is also built by being a "real person" who is able to be authentic, let their guard down, and make the client feel comfortable. The client, in turn, may be more willing to be casual and authentic as well. Trust is also built by paraphrasing what the client says to show understanding, remembering the details, and working through challenges with a sense of optimism and humor. Building a trust relationship can take a great deal of effort, and it can be lost quickly. As Warren Buffett famously said, "It takes 20 years to build a reputation and five minutes to ruin it. If you think about that, you'll do things differently."

Once you have established trust, you will begin to see a melding of the personal and professional relationship. You'll be more empathetic and start seeing work challenges through the lens of how it impacts your client personally – how they struggle over how these challenges impact their employees, their family, their mental health. You'll also watch some of the skepticism about your motives recede. Your client won't worry about whether you are just trying to win more business, they will begin to view you as a confidant invested in their success.

Cassandra Isbell, a director at BDO, is renowned for building lasting client relationships. She has received encomiums from clients extolling her virtues, and BDO even wrote an article upholding Cassandra as the exemplar in building *lasting* client relationships. When I asked Cassandra to impart some of her wisdom, she told me, "The key to building lasting, with an emphasis on lasting, client relationships is determining their long-term goals rather than what is immediately in front of you. This comes from active listening and taking time to truly understand their motivations – is it their legacy? having an impact? building something? Listen to everything that they are trying to say and pull these disparate pieces together." Cassandra emphasized the importance of active listening over the course of the many forums, small group and one-on-one meetings, and informal conversations. "Abide by the 80/20 rule. You should be doing only 20% of the talking and 80% of the listening. When you are listening, you are learning, and the right question can help you learn far more than anything you present to the client."

Clients often appreciate being educated and being given options. Part of building a lasting relationship is to provide them with choices, educate them on the choices, and make a recommendation based on your understanding of the problem. While it's not always easy, you have to accept that the choice is theirs and that you are serving as a consigliere. If your recommendation is not adopted (and it likely will not always be), then be prepared to work with the client to implement the option they selected, provide continued guidance, and prepare for any risks (and avoid "I told you so" if/when their decision does not work out). Part of being a consultant is being a guide and providing a roadmap with multiple avenues.

Your client is not a title or position, they are an individual with unique expectations and motivations, and they are your collaborator. Building a lasting relationship is demonstrating that you are on a shared journey that involves defining the problem (where you are going); are consistently considering stops along the way and how to best get there (helping them build their roadmap); and are able to share insights and recommendations from other journeys, provide tools, templates, and techniques or modify or even co-create solutions.

Building client relationships is about facilitating high-quality experiences. Clients are naturally skeptical of someone "invading" their office or being a temporary part of their organization. Each interaction provides an opportunity to create value, develop an authentic relationship, and show that you are trying to "do the right thing." This right thing is not selling more business or promoting one way of doing things. It's molding methodologies and bending best practices to meet the client's needs.

A consultant needs to earn the right to give advice. You must demonstrate that you understand the client's situation, motivations, and desires, and build their confidence that you are coming to them with this perspective in mind. When giving advice, learn which approach works for your client. For some, it is showing empathy and an understanding of where they are coming from. For others, it is using those teaching skills through deductive or inductive reasoning. For deductive reasoning, you may start with a hypothesis with a number of assumptions and then test that hypothesis together. For inductive reasoning, you may use the Socratic method, asking questions around empirical observations and sharpening those questions to reach a general approach or solution. Leading the client to a solution through guided questions, awareness of their own observations, or inception can help a client reach the conclusion on their own. Cassandra also emphasized the importance of learning the client's background and jargon. "When you know where they come from and what language is comfortable to them, you can put things in those terms and build analogies. One client had over 20 years of experience in a metropolitan police department, and so when I present things to him, I do so using that language to build comparisons and help shape the recommendation."

Cassandra shared insights into how you know when you are building a lasting client relationship: "You know that you have moved to trusted advisor when the client starts actively seeking your expertise for areas above and beyond your role. When they start asking you for advice around hiring, career goals, their performance, or seeking your honest opinion, you know you have secured trusted advisor status." Cassandra cautioned that this status can be lost when you start to "confuse sympathy with empathy. You can be empathetic while also remaining objective. When you become too close to the client and start to cloud things with sympathy then you start to lose your independence and trust."

****

When I joined a highly visible, high-pressure project that was the client's second attempt (after a failed effort with another consulting company), our team faced a lot of skepticism. The client was already on high alert from the previous effort, had little patience for ramp-up time, and wanted to see immediate value-add. Our team reviewed our internal research and initiated meetings (not too many) that were targeted on a specific ask or based on a particular theme. We acknowledged that the client was facing pressure and operating under a time crunch, and that we were sensitive to the lessons learned from the past effort. We asked the client questions about their expectations and paraphrased these statements back to them. In subsequent meetings and email correspondence, we let them know that we heard them by highlighting why we were doing something. Over time, they began to shed their armor. Part of this came from our acknowledgment of their concerns, part of this came from a divide-and-conquer strategy where we segmented communications so that a particular person could have a more one-on-one tailored response to a particular stakeholder, and part of this also came from personally revealing ourselves and likewise learning about the clients' selves in our meetings. Eventually, the client began to see us as a collaborator and began to have more candid conversations about the challenges they were experiencing, started co-creating actions and next steps with us, and become more invested in us as teammates supporting their success. Ultimately, as our relationship grew, the prospects for project success and future partnerships also grew.

****

During my career supporting various projects, I've continued to maintain contact with former clients. I'm happy to say that many of these client-consultant relationships have turned into friendships. Several have blossomed into regular check-ins where we share updates on our favorite television shows, ask for guidance on work challenges we are facing, and even sometimes talk politics (and I don't even talk politics with some of my closest family members!). We've celebrated life milestones, supported causes that matter to each other, and helped serve as members of each other's PBAs. These relationships are based on trust and candor and not about developing business (although they could translate into business down the road). Many have been forged by being in the trenches together and letting our guard down, stepping outside of work-speak, and being authentic and even vulnerable.

Jim Riddick is a former client with whom I have built one such lasting relationship. Jim has shared with me that initially he was skeptical of me and my team, but felt we were able to quickly establish "mutual trust, which helped us communicate, integrate, and operate more effectively." What it took to establish that trust was our team being "reliable, responsive, and showing that we were competently and effectively working together." That trust was also built by us showing Jim "that we were looking out for him and trying to do the right thing, even when we disagreed." We approached challenges from Jim's perspective and presented things in the light of how we felt it could impact him and his responsibilities. Jim felt grateful for this perspective and eventually made several compromises based on it ("even though chances were that I was right," he joked). Establishing this trust early on by showing that we were trying to better understand the client perspective, were working effectively as a team, and were interested in doing what was right for the client helped fortify our relationship. This allowed us to work far more effectively together and continue our relationship long after we moved onto another project.

✶✶✶✶✶✶✶✶

One of the best resources on building lasting client relationships is *The Trusted Advisor*[21] by David Maister, Charles Green, and Robert Galford. This book provides a thoughtful, thorough, and reader-friendly way to view your role as consultant and how to cultivate and navigate relationships with clients.

37

HOW DO YOU MANAGE A TEAM?

In this second 3–5 year stage in your career, you'll likely have the opportunity to take on more responsibility or even directly manage a team. Just as I highlighted earlier the qualities to look for in a team and how you can contribute to a successful team dynamic, you may now have the opportunity to build a strong team culture. There are a number of benefits to managing an effective team – productivity, achievement, recognition, and relationships that extend beyond the project.

When I talked with Tiffany Yang about her experience working with teams, she noted that a good team provides (1) personal and professional support; (2) focus that leads to clear roles, responsibilities, and achievement; and (3) continuous progress and improvement. Tiffany went on to share what made one of her team experiences so impactful and why – even after members have left for different projects, firms, and careers – this team continues to provide lessons for all of its members. In her team, Tiffany found that a diversity of thought and experience was important. Team members were able to share experiences and perspectives, which helped others learn and grow, and enabled teammates to self-organize around their strengths.

Tiffany also highlighted the importance of creating an environment of mutual respect:

> Teams produce exceptional results when all members feel supported and heard. Each team member brings different strengths and perspectives, but this diversity is null if team members aren't given space to show, apply, and learn from them with their teams. Though it's impossible to include each person's opinion into every decision, it's hugely important to ensure that teams provide a venue for collective discussion so that all members feel that they are continuously contributing to the group's success.

Managers need to provide space for people to share their thoughts, experiences, and approach, and they must share their own reasoning behind a decision. This transparency fosters respect, and while teammates may not always agree, it at least helps them better understand the thought process behind a decision and helps them learn from your approach (whether or not it is the right one). This does not mean that a leader abdicates their decision-making. It means they listen, learn, and understand the concerns and feedback of the team before moving ahead with a decision. Tiffany felt that the team leader "shouldn't have both the question and the answer; their goal is to unify the team around an objective and provide additional support, action, or top cover to get there. Likewise, they should be impartial arbiters among team members and between the team and the client." The "top cover" piece is especially important. As a manager, you need to publicly support your team and privately coach them. Teammates need to feel that they have room to breathe, make mistakes, and learn from these mistakes. They need to feel like their manager is on their side and is shielding them and supporting them rather than throwing them under the bus.

When I asked one of my mentors, Dave Brant, about how he managed teams of consultants at Deloitte and BDO and oversaw the 2,500-employee Naval Criminal Investigative Service (NCIS), he described how adept managers are able to identify and apply people's skills to areas where they can excel:

> The most important thing depending on the size, technical skills, reach, is an ability to recognize that there are different members of your team with different personalities, skill sets, and capability levels. Recognize and set expectations that are fair to each team member. The more successful leaders leverage, value, and motivate people who are going to reach different heights and levels of success and are able to use their understanding of that person to shape their contributions to the team.

I've highlighted empathy as an attribute of a good teammate, and perhaps this is most important when building a team culture. Building personal relationships with your team, understanding that there may be outside factors affecting their work, and picking up the slack or temporarily re-distributing the workload when a teammate is down can foster greater comfort, commitment, and productivity. As previously noted, Tiffany Yang saw this as part of her team:

> Teammates bring their best, and their team can expect them to know

(and vocalize) when they need to take a break to recalibrate. Time off to take care of personal appointments and needs decreases individual stress and reaffirms that their team is present to provide support when they need it. And, when (not if) team members are having a tough day or going through difficult life circumstances, space, empathy, and understanding allow them to return with a clear head, versus lashing out at teammates or ignoring an issue and allowing it to persist, interfering with their ability to work. Teammates who give each other time graciously will find that, rather than abusing it, devoted teammates will want to do the same for others.

Another aspect of this is having confidence in teammates – superpowers, strengths, and weaknesses. When you believe in your teammates, they cannot help but believe in themselves.

I can hear some managers reading this muttering with skepticism. Part of managing your team is knowing their motivations, capabilities, and limitations. Providing room to grow and autonomy can help build trust and enhance productivity. That autonomy depends on your team's strengths, capabilities, and limitations, and you may need to be more directive when teammates are hitting their limits, learning a new skill, facing a new experience, or not meeting expectations. When working through challenges as a team, do not confuse validation with agreement. You can validate and recognize someone's perspective without necessarily agreeing with it. This can be done by asking questions to better understand their viewpoint and then sharing your reasoning and perspective.

Tiffany shared her perspective on a type of project that you may face and the outcome of a successful team effort:

> One project involved getting a federal government agency accustomed to reporting data on a recurring basis. While it sounds simple, this was no easy feat: the agency was accustomed to collecting data for individual recordkeeping requirements, not reporting the data in a formalized venue to their supervisor and peers; and even more importantly, they were not comfortable enough with data to extrapolate point-in-time numbers to long-term trends and forecasts.

> Because of their discomfort, midlevel managers were reluctant to begin the task of formulating regular data briefings. My team developed the

foundation for the briefing – the briefing template – but also clearly stated objectives and desired outcomes of the briefing. With that, members of the team each took responsibility for guiding two or three managers on how to select data to present, how to present the data to prompt a decision, and how to introduce rigor in data-collection procedures to ensure that data would be collected continuously, accurately, and in a timely fashion. My team met often to voice the questions and concerns they'd heard from their managers, brainstorm solutions, refine templates and messaging, and agree on the path forward.

Over the course of eight briefings, managers went from presenting inventories to trends, and one-way briefings began to take the form of discourse, with peers offering suggestions to improve, their own data and staff to augment initial analysis, and more open discussions on trends and necessary action, based on data in multiple areas.

Managers (and their supervisors) all recognized the progress they had made, which was a huge boon to our team's confidence and reputation.

****

Team efforts start with creating an environment where teammates trust each other, are comfortable, and feel like they can simultaneously leverage their strengths while also learning and growing. Often, when the client sees the team operating in sync, being dependable and reliable, and building on each other's efforts, they become more likely to engage and be a part of the effort. This fosters a virtuous cycle that can lead to greater confidence, team growth, and an enhanced reputation. Perhaps most importantly, it can contribute to lasting relationships between teammates and the client. I still get emails, texts, and calls years later from the client highlighting how well our team worked together, and our team, while on other projects, working for different companies, and even, in some cases, in different industries, continues to keep in touch and share what is going on in our personal and professional lives. A little upfront work creating a strong team culture and ongoing vigilance and support pays deep personal and professional dividends.

38

HOW DO YOU RESPOND TO A CLIENT NOT TAKING YOUR RECOMMENDATION?

There are going to be times when you work overtime on the "perfect" recommendation validated by benchmarking, forecasting, Monte Carlo simulations, regression analysis, stakeholder interviews – the works. You've carefully crafted the recommendation and are convinced that it will be a game-changer for the client. And . . .They don't take it. Now what? First, recognize that there is no "perfect" recommendation. No matter how invested you are in the client and how strong the trusted advisor relationship you have built, your recommendation will not always be accepted or implemented. While this can be frustrating and it can feel like you have put in time and effort for nothing, you have to recognize that the ultimate decision resides with the client. When this happens, make sure to: (1) reframe your recommendation, (2) support your team, and (3) show the value that your team delivered.

REFRAME YOUR RECOMMENDATION

Consider why your recommendation may not have been taken. Are there internal politics? Is there a resource challenge? Did you not effectively communicate? Ask questions to better understand why a recommendation is being ignored and incorporate new information to adapt your recommendation.

Recommendations should be aligned to business objectives. Showing how yours aligns with the client's business objectives can build a roadmap for the future. Clients sometimes need to better understand the alternatives. Presenting clients with several options and providing them with the pros and cons of each recommendation can help them to better evaluate their choices.

Perhaps you misjudged your client's communication style or presented the recommendation with the wrong decision-maker in mind. Get to know the decision-maker's style – do they respond better to a vision of how the recommendation leads to the future state? To the risk of not implementing it? Stories? Data? Benchmarking against the competition? Sometimes you may need to take a second attempt at reframing so that the client better understands the recommendation's impact and feels like they are making the best choice.

SUPPORT YOUR TEAM

When you have lived a project for weeks or months, it can be a kick in the gut when you have to reframe or redo work. Acknowledge that this is a learning experience and an opportunity to capture lessons learned. Recognize also that you need to protect your team. Review the scope of the contract and ensure that you have met its standards. Make sure that the final presentations and deliverables are documented and that both clients and your company have the documentation permanently stored. This protects you from finger-pointing and blame from the client if the alternative they chose does not meet their anticipated results. Document the risks that you foresee if they choose an alternative path and see if they might consider counsel on the approach they have chosen. This allows you to show that you have raised red flags and have tried to mitigate potential risks. Finally, make sure to have a conversation with the client to affirm your commitment to their success and the value that you have brought to their organization.

SHOW YOUR VALUE

Even if a recommendation has not been accepted, show that your time and client's money has not been wasted. Highlight key findings and takeaways from your analysis and consider how these lessons learned can be repurposed. Provide the client with a roadmap of how they can incorporate your analysis into their actions. Reaffirm that you are invested in their success and highlight how your team has supported them.

****

I've experienced many rejected recommendations, and each one has allowed me to learn crucial lessons and provided an opportunity to better meet the client's needs. One example that immediately comes to mind was a recommendation on a training approach, which was aligned with best practices and would simplify how training was conducted. The client had already made several changes to the scope and did not believe this change to training strategy was necessary. We documented this with the team, and when we delivered the training the way the client had proposed, the client was dissatisfied. Lo and behold! – they recommended that we update their approach to reflect some of our initial recommendations. Our team quickly adapted, documented the changes, and delivered the revised training. While there was tension with the client, there was also appreciation that had we listened to their feedback, responded quickly, and were able to repurpose material from the original training to help meet their needs. They also appreciated that we did not complain or follow up with an "I told you so." Ultimately, our response enabled us to deliver the project, strengthen our rapport, and build a lasting relationship by winning proposals for future work.

39

HOW DO YOU HANDLE BURNOUT?

Deadlines. Milestones. Deliverables. Meeting upon meeting. Proposals. Managing risks. Too often, the onus of responsibility placed on individuals breaks them down mentally and physically. We've all likely witnessed or experienced burnout at some stage. The World Health Organization describes it as "resulting from chronic workplace stress that has not been successfully managed." Symptoms include "feelings of energy depletion or exhaustion, increased mental distance from one's job, or feelings of negativism or cynicism related to one's job; and reduced professional efficacy." Burnout can be, and often is, collective.

Health risks of burnout include increased risk of coronary disease, which can contribute to type II diabetes and biological aging. There are also neurological implications – less attention to detail, less capacity for decision-making, and challenges with recall, memory, and emotional regulation. Burnout also tends to affect those around us as they suffer "compassion fatigue" or experience this stress along with us. Beyond the physical and mental costs are the economic costs – burnout costs organizations an estimated $120 billion–$190 billion a year![22]

Managing burnout can not only help you live a happier and healthier life, but also enable you to retain (happier and healthier) talent and deliver your best work.

IDENTIFYING BURNOUT

Burnout can occur at several levels – individual, team, and organizational. At the individual level, certain people may be more predisposed to burnout as a result of their coping mechanisms, support network, and personality characteristics. You or your teammates may suffer from perfectionism and have anxiety over making a mistake or delivering an imperfect product (see chapter 26 on imposter syndrome). Burnout can also take hold at the team level and can escalate during times of tight timelines, when team dynamics or culture impact the ability to successfully complete work, and when there are not clear lines of communication or people feel uncomfortable taking risks.

Knowing people's burnout vulnerabilities and what causes burnout in them can help. Stanford Hospital recently instituted a quick two-minute quiz (https://www.skylyte.io/self-assessment) to help people identify the factors contributing to their own burnout. This assessment sets out 12 questions on how you approach problems and deal with setbacks. It then provides you with your typology, your strengths, recommended actions, risks, and how you could impact your team. Full-blown burnout takes an average of 14 months to two years to recover from, and being able to identify and manage it early on can substantially reduce the cost and length of interventions. Be self-aware of your typology and know your team!

OVERCOME BURNOUT

To reduce the risk of individual burnout, create an environment where it is acceptable to learn, grow, and leverage others. Establish support systems within your team and advocate for resources from your firm. Many firms offer stress relievers and tips to help make the workplace more tenable during those high-stress times. As a leader, it is vital that you use your emotional intelligence to identify when someone may be feeling down, be empathetic, and be aware of resources to counteract stress. This also goes for you. Ensure you have a support network that allows you to vent and take breaks to recharge – whether its practicing mindfulness, meditating, exercising, or scheduling a mental health day. Set the tone for your team and model that burnout is something that needs to be actively managed.

At the team level, foster a culture where you and your team can be open, transparent, and vulnerable (see chapter 37, on managing teams). Early intervention is critical and so setting this environment up front, proactively reviewing the project schedule and highlighting areas of potential high stress (major deliverables or milestones), and having systems and structures in place to alleviate burnout will help prepare you for success.

The effort to manage individual and team burnout must be constant over time. Poor relationships with direct managers account for nearly 75% of turnover[23]; thus, you play a critical role in retaining your staff, particularly during high-stress situations. Transparency and fairness are also key elements in combating burnout. Distributing work fairly, being open and honest, and recognizing unconscious biases that may influence your decisions can help you to better lead your team and avoid burnout.

Part of overcoming burnout is establishing keystones of resilience within the team. The Four Pillars of Resilience in the *Stanford Social Innovation Review* article "Burnout from an Organizational Perspective"[24] provide an overview of the dynamic that you want to foster in your teams to avoid burnout:

- **Self-Awareness:** Encouraging team members to know their strengths, triggers, and to be vulnerable enough to share these with the team
- **Autonomy:** Balancing independence with support so that team members can do their best work
- **Structured Rest and Relaxation:** Ensuring time for rest is protected and encouraged and that the workload is evenly distributed
- **Community:** Establishing a culture of collaboration, comfort, and trust so that teammates can better work together to accomplish goals

****

Burnout has an outsized impact on our own and our team's ability to deliver excellent work. Being mindful of how burnout manifests itself, affects you and those around you, and actively managing it can help you retain team members, keep productivity and morale high, and accomplish your goals.

40
WHEN IS IT TIME TO LEAVE YOUR FIRM?

At some point, you may hit a crossroads when you need to determine whether you stay within the comfortable confines of your firm or pursue seemingly greener pastures. This can be a career-defining move and an extremely difficult decision. In your current firm, you have likely built up a thorough understanding of the internal systems and processes, established a strong network, and know what is expected to advance your career. Starting fresh at a new firm, you will need to build new relationships, learn the processes and politics, and establish credibility and your reputation. I've had countless conversations with consultants evaluating whether or not to make a move. Consider opportunities for (1) career trajectory, (2) growth, (3) work-life balance, and (4) new prospects.

CAREER TRAJECTORY

At some point, you may begin to plateau. Perhaps your firm can only support a limited number of people at your target level (director, partner) – revenue growth may have stalled, you might be unable to meet certain target metrics, or, as a result of immense competition, the expectations for promotion have shifted and this moving target has become ceaselessly challenging to meet. When your career trajectory seems to have entered quicksand, you may seek that vine to pull yourself out. It may take the form of a conversation with a mentor or advisor, a transition to a new role, or acceptance of your current position. In any case, you will need to evaluate whether you can jump-start your career internally or whether a move can provide you with the title or fresh space to galvanize you.

One consultant at a major firm was stuck in the dreaded "senior manager trap." This is often considered one of the most challenging roles in consulting. As a senior manager, you face the full gamut of challenges of upper-middle management. You still have extensive client delivery responsibilities and are probably leading projects day-to-day. But now you also have business development expectations where you may need to manage proposals and bring in a set amount of business. Finally, you are also expected to contribute to the firm, mentor others, and lead firm initiatives. Where does one find the time to do all of this well? The senior manager shared that after succeeding on all stages and putting in serious overtime leveraging one of his relationships, serving as the architect for a major proposal that his firm ultimately won, and effectively leading client delivery, he hit a wall. He felt he had done everything he could have done to get promoted and was still told that it was a few years away. With a young family, he had to decide whether or not to sustain high performance in this role for a few years in the hope that he would advance or to take a leadership role elsewhere and use his skills on a smaller scale. Ultimately, he elected to take a leadership role at a smaller firm. This move gave him greater autonomy, a higher title, and directly tied his compensation to his ability to bring in business.

GROWTH

At some point, your job may become routine. While there are advantages to knowing what to expect day in, day-out, this can become monotonous – and the sameness can also limit your long-term prospects. Growth and learning can be halted when you are pigeonholed into a certain position or have built such strong relationships with a client or project team that you are kept there by necessity. There may be ways to continue to learn internally and externally, even if the day-to-day project does not change. For instance, you may take on leadership roles in your community, participate in thought leadership efforts, or lead internal initiatives. You may also elect to pursue a certification to build or extend your skills. But at some point, you may come to that crossroads of deciding whether or not you are growing enough to be a viable leader in your firm or are better off hitting the refresh button.

Two very talented consultants were confronted with this same question. They had built a solid relationship with the client, were respected by the project team and firm, and by necessity, were pigeonholed on the same client. Both advanced and elected to lead internal firm initiatives, earned certifications, and sought additional responsibilities on the project team. Both were faced with the comfort level versus growth trade-off quandary. One of them, on the verge of a promotion, accepted an offer with another firm so that she could build stronger skill sets and prepare to manage a team. The other appreciated the comfort and stability that her role afforded her. Her relatively steady job enabled her to focus valuable brain space elsewhere and leave work at the office. She stayed with the firm, was promoted, and continued to evaluate her options. Both made the decision that was right for them.

WORK-LIFE BALANCE

Competition, targets, and the drive to advance can take up increasingly more time. Many people advance by showing they are meeting the expectations demanded by the role above them for an extended period of time while also sustaining high performance in their current role. This learning curve while sustaining high performance can eat into your personal obligations. You may find yourself spending more time writing proposals, putting out project fires, or attending firm networking or "mandatory optional" events to demonstrate that you have met certain corporate contribution metrics. All of this translates into time away from your family, friends, and community. Many are driven by competition or comparison to their peers or idols, performance targets, and the desire to make a slam dunk case for promotion. Others may feel burned out or may have shifted their priorities. At some point, the corporate ladder has become less enticing and they may value work-life balance over career advancement.

A consultant at a major firm was grappling with this. He was at the manager level and on track for promotion to senior manager. Looking ahead, he foresaw the dreaded senior manager trap and considered whether he wanted to take on the additional workload or to seek a role that enabled him to meet expectations without cutting into family time. He chose to look for a company where the competition, expectations, and time commitment expected of a senior manager were less cumbersome: "Once I hit senior manager, I'll need to deliver excellent client service, bring in $2 million in business, and attend firm events, and I'm just not sure if I want to do that. I don't want to be writing proposals on nights and weekends. I want to spend time with my kids." As you advance in your career, your priorities may also advance and evolve. You'll need to look at the road ahead and determine what trade-offs you are willing to make.

NEW PROSPECTS

Consulting often opens opportunities for ongoing learning, whether working with diverse teams, ramping up and leading different project engagements, or supporting different clients or industries. Each offers a refresh and a chance to learn and grow. Sometimes the pull of another opportunity becomes too great to resist, luring you from your current role. Perhaps it's the chance to learn a new skill, industry, or specialize in a particular area.

Perhaps it's the chance to take on greater responsibility elsewhere. Perhaps it's the chance to go internal and apply your consulting skills to only one company – the company that hires you. Perhaps it's the chance to carve out you own mini empire by going independent. All of these options provide their own advantages and drawbacks.

****

Each of these factors contributed in part to my decision to make a career transition. At the time, I was receiving continuous affirmation that I was on the partner track for the firm that I was currently at. We had built an amazing team of talented and diverse individuals. I had built strong relationships with a client and continued to deliver solid service while leading firm initiatives, getting involved in my community through nonprofit board leadership, publishing thought leadership pieces, and earning certifications. And despite my involvement in these initiatives and activities and my career trajectory toward partner, I had a very comfortable work-life balance.

But I had doubts as well. I evaluated whether making partner was feasible, given the practice's organic growth prospects, and wondered what it would take for the firm to support another partner. It could be a long haul and while partner was my initial goal, my other priorities began to become more important. Learning and growth were important to me, and while I was crafting opportunities for that elsewhere, the day-to-day job did not always afford them to me. Conversations with leadership seemed to yield dead-ends or roadblocks. The allure of a new opportunity that would test and develop my skills with distinct clients, enable me to further develop expertise, and extend my experience across a different business line was compelling. Ultimately, ongoing growth and learning exceeded my desire for a potential partner title and opened doors to greater future opportunities.

LIFE AFTER CONSULTING

By this stage, you may have developed a few 3–5 year plans and are considering your next steps. You've built strong relationships, developed leadership skills, and have become adept at solving complex problems. One of the great things about consulting is that it opens doors and can provide an array of options. You might want to keep advancing up the corporate ladder with an eye to partner and are considering how to position yourself for that milestone. Perhaps you are interested in becoming a "free agent" and becoming an independent consultant. You'll need to consider how you market yourself and leverage established client relationships to maintain an ongoing book of business. Perhaps you are considering starting your own practice and will need to build business and expertise to sustain a team and grow an organization. Perhaps you're feeling the burn of constantly building business and overseeing new projects and are looking for more consistent in-house consulting work for one company. You may also be looking to stay connected to consulting and work in-house in an internal operations role. With the vast array of experience and war stories that you have to share, you may look into becoming a professor of practice who shares their knowledge with budding consultants-to-be.

At various stages of my career, I have considered (and continue to consider) all these options and more. I've had countless conversations and gained insights from my PBAs and friends in industry who have also considered life after consulting (LAC), or even taken the leap of faith and left their firms. The reasons vary – career plateau, opportunity to learn, chance to go into business on their own, more money, more flexibility, etc. What's important is that you'll have to prioritize what matters most for you, evaluate your path forward, and determine what makes the most sense at this stage in your career.

Consulting offers a diverse portfolio of options and the option value that consulting affords is just one premium of this career. Career change is rarely linear, and you should expect the path to life after consulting to be circuitous. Imagine your divergent selves and possible futures and accept that plans are made to be updated. You've developed the tools to be successful and hold the keys to your future. Now, like any skilled consultant, you need to execute!

41

DO YOU WANT TO MAKE PARTNER?

Making partner is just one of several avenues in your career roadmap. While your title does not define you and how successful you are in your career, the status, salary, and ability to lead that come with a partner designation could contribute to your overall happiness. Be wary though – as they say, more money, more problems. While I've noted earlier that the path to partner starts on day one, this can be somewhat ambiguous. Paths to partner can be convoluted, and it depends on timing, hustle, and taking advantage of opportunities in front of you. That consultant who started overseas before rising to a partner in the New York office of a top tier firm applied the famous Mike Tyson quote to the process: "Everyone has a plan until they get punched in the face." Hopefully, you are not taking too many punches on your path to partner, but the point is valid. Plans can hit a variety of roadblocks – personality differences, lack of practice or firm growth, changing priorities. The important thing to realize is that you may take a circuitous route to partner – or may ultimately decide that there are more important things than becoming partner. This partner shared that while there is no formula or playbook, delivering excellent work, building relationships, and having that "hustle factor" can help get you closer to the holy grail. As a partner, you will focus less on delivery (unless on a highly visible, controversial, or at-risk project) and more on sales, strategy, and mentoring and coaching. Your relationships, emotional intelligence, and communication skills will be a key part of your influence and role.

When I asked Yashomati Bachul Koul about their role as a principal at Kearney and whether or not this was something they deliberately and methodically progressed toward, Koul shared these insights:

> Anyone who aspires for partner should really ask themselves why: Why do you want to be a principal or a partner? The industry has a really interesting way of making you feel like if you don't stay and make that next level, then you have somehow failed. It has this aura of a very

exclusive club, and you don't want to ever leave it. But it is not for everyone...and that is ok. Many people then start to redefine success by consulting terms rather than by their own terms. The second you define success from terms other than your own, you face the possibility that you will always be chasing, and never achieving, happiness. It is an incredibly demanding job, and there is not always work-life balance. But if you love what you do, you can find the energy to make it through the challenging periods. Personalize your definition of success to be inclusive of work, life, family, community, etc. A job title alone should never be your lone definition of success.

For those who do make it to partner, there are some key benefits, including (1) status, (2) compensation, and (3) flexibility.

STATUS

In many firms, partner is hallowed ground. Those who reach that designation have slain dragons (competitors), led (business) conquests, rescued those (projects and teammates) in distress; and bards (business gurus, writers, alumni, consulting disciples) tell tales of their victories. Yes, this is hyperbolic, but partner does give you a valued position in company lore. To reach this destination, you likely have brought in a lot of business, mentored and coached talented consultants who themselves have had meteoric careers, and successfully led high-impact firm initiatives. The partner title is treated with reverence, and this status extends beyond just your firm. A fabled few rise through the ranks to meet this milestone. Again, while your job title does not define you, becoming partner does validate your hard work and will signal respect for your achievements. When you reach this designation, do not forget the countless people who helped you reach this peak and remember that you now serve as a role model to other aspiring consultants, managers, directors, partners, and leaders in the firm.

COMPENSATION

With the partner title comes an increase in salary. This will vary depending on the firm, and where you truly see your compensation increase is during your high-performing years. In down years, your total compensation might only be slightly higher than what directors bring in. In very successful years (and if you lead a particularly profitable practice), you can see your total compensation substantially increase. As noted in chapter 14 (on negotiation), compensation can extend beyond just monetary value. Firms may have benefits exclusively for partners, such as club memberships, attendance at lucrative conferences, corporate spending accounts, and a broad range of other allowances. Money certainly isn't everything, but this compensation is certainly a key benefit.

FLEXIBILITY

Establishing yourself as a partner in the firm provides greater opportunities for leadership and autonomy. While you and the firm will always have certain targets, you'll have greater control over how you achieve them. For instance, if you hustle hard or have built a solid book of business and relationships over the years, you may be able to hit your targets earlier and then can decide whether or not to scale back your workload. You'll likely have greater flexibility over your schedule – choosing when to come into the office, where and when to take business meetings, and whom to delegate certain tasks to. Part of that control comes with overseeing aspiring partners who may have gravitated toward your sphere of influence. Guiding, mentoring, and leveraging these talented leaders give you a choice of whether to continue to advance or take more of a delegator-in-chief approach to dividing labor and achieving balance.

****

While becoming partner affords considerable benefits, you are going to have to make trade-offs to reach the promised land. These include (1) managing work-life balance, (2) increased competition, and (3) career obstacles.

MANAGING WORK-LIFE BALANCE

Becoming partner can be a perilous path that requires more than just excelling in a 9–5 role. Aspiring partners are often pounding the pavement for business development leads, networking and building relationships, contributing to thought leadership efforts, successfully leading high impact and visible firm initiatives, and mentoring, coaching, and managing high-performing teams. For those whose path to partner starts on day one, it takes a lot of intentional planning, preparation, and deliberate action to reach this level. This can come at the expense of your personal life. You may find your professional life creeping into, or even overwhelming your personal life as you spend evenings and weekends attending conferences, writing proposals, networking, and providing feedback on deliverables. This pattern often needs to be sustained for years, and as your life changes and priorities shift, you'll need to make critical decisions around where you draw the boundaries around work-life balance.

The consultant who turned his overseas internship into a partnership position in under 10 years shared some of the trade-offs of becoming partner:

> It may appear that partners work less (and some do), but the reality is that folks that rise through the ranks lose one of the best perks of consulting: the project-based nature or work. Post-MBA consultants can push hard while on an engagement but can take a few days "on the beach" (being unstaffed) or take a literal vacation to disconnect before the next opportunity comes along. Many firms offer perks such as additional unpaid leave, externship opportunities, etc. At the same time, partners never really stop working. They have to actively stay in touch with their network to market themselves and the firm, take business development calls when some folks just try to get free advice/information, work on tailoring proposals, be partially with the team on the engagement (while selling future work in parallel), and last, but not least, deal with any follow up questions after the project is wrapped and the team is already re-staffed. Needless to say, they take their laptops with them for every vacation and keep their phones handy on the weekends. Work does not truly stop and is infused with each partner's life – so you have to love what you do, not just to be happy, but also to be successful in your career as a senior leader.

COMPETITION

Not everyone reaches the top of the pyramid and many are vying for that select role. Countless consultants climb and claw their way to reach the top, sometimes at the expense of relationships, reputation, and rest. To achieve partner, you need to excel in bringing in business, managing teams, and leading firm or industry initiatives (the vaunted triple threat). While you can get creative in each of these efforts and may even be able to craft your own efforts, there are often fixed opportunities to get involved. You might get priority based on your skills, experiences, and network and sometimes this requires long-term positioning before you're selected for a partner-building opportunity.

Being on the partner track can be a precarious balance. Several high-performing senior managers, including myself, at my former firm were vying for partner knowing that there were likely limited opportunities to achieve it. While we worked effectively as a team, I think each of us also looked at each other with a wary eye. If we saw someone leading a firm initiative, one of us would step up, take on more responsibility, and lead another firm effort. This sometimes became a race to the top and it did not always foster the best working dynamic. At some point, a leader in my firm even pulled me aside to let me know that my efforts to lead multiple initiatives and share how our team was contributing to practice growth might be alienating other members of the firm, setting unrealistic expectations for everyone to achieve, and even causing other colleagues to view my motives with skepticism. It's a difficult balance. Make sure you are contributing to your firm for the right reasons – firm growth, mentoring, coaching, and helping others achieve – and not for your own personal achievements.

OVERCOMING OBSTACLES

Building the network, knowledge, and skills to be a partner takes time and is a long-term investment outside of your traditional working hours. This often begins in your 20s, with the heavy push for partner coming in your 30s or 40s. With this being peak parenting time, your priorities often come into conflict. Attend your child's dance recital or soccer match or attend a potentially lucrative business meeting? Spend your weekend working on a proposal or spending time with your family? Put off starting a family to push for partner beforehand? Too often, consultants put too much stock into becoming partner and view this as the pinnacle of their careers. Most put in all those extra hours only to never reach this stage.

I've seen consultants take different strategies in seeking the holy grail. One is to have their spouse's career take a backseat to their own; this is often a conversation between the couple where the one pursuing partner acknowledges that they may require more time focused on their profession and the other finds a lighter role where they can focus more on the family. Another strategy is prioritizing their time on the path to partner and outsourcing errands, chores, and jobs that pull them away from their single-minded path. Many consultants do this effectively – what's paying someone else $100 or so for two hours of yard work when those two hours could be repurposed to a business meeting yielding a multimillion-dollar contract? Finally, there's downshifting to a smaller firm. Consultants at large firms may ultimately find the path too perilous or the competition too stiff and may ultimately downsize to a firm that might have lower expectations or greater flexibility for someone to reach partner level.

****

When I asked that consultant who first worked overseas about pursuing the path to partner, he suggested that anyone seeking partner should take a

T-approach when they are starting out. This means that you start with more broad experience where you take on different projects, challenge yourself, and learn as much as you can (the horizontal line in the T). He warned that those who try too hard to be perfect risk missing opportunities for learning or growth that could position you better down the road. Once you have gained that solid base, then you can specialize (the vertical line in the T). A second great piece of advice was that plans are meant to be updated. A firm, business line, or office may no longer be the right fit for you for a variety of reasons – cultural differences, project opportunities, personality differences. If your position becomes untenable, move on and do great work elsewhere rather than be miserable at your current firm. Being unhappy will prevent you from doing your best work, which prevents you from achieving your goals. Third, cater to your strengths. As I've discussed earlier, you get far higher ROI from leveraging your strengths rather than developing your weaknesses. If you excel at building relationships, then identify opportunities to get yourself in front of clients and company leaders. If strategy is your superpower, participate in firm initiatives when you can craft strategy. If you are a spreadsheet jockey, conduct analytics that highlight opportunities for your firm.

This consultant's path to partner started with a plan with numerous twists and turns. Many work their way up through the ranks at one firm. His career started with an internship overseas at a top-tier firm followed by a full-time offer. After two years overseas, he transferred internally to the New York City office. He quickly saw that this office was not the right fit and moved to a boutique firm where he could grow quickly, take on added responsibility, and craft his career around his own consulting superpowers. When the boutique was acquired by an established firm, he continued to be a go-to resource, a utility person who hustled hard and found his niche and quickly rose to partner. While his original plan may have been to climb the ladder at one firm, he ultimately recognized that there were alternatives routes and adjusted his plan, as consultants do, to new information.

****

Getting to partner is certainly something to be celebrated and is an amazing accomplishment, but it should not be the peak of your career. It is something you can aspire for, strategize for, and work toward. It can be a powerful motivator and something that makes you better. However, recognize that your priorities may shift over time and that partner does not define how successful your career has been. Countless consultants have had, and will have, very successful careers without reaching partner. Others have made partner at one firm only to leave and start their own firm or join as a partner elsewhere. There are many paths, and partner is just one among many.

42

WHAT OTHER OPPORTUNITIES EXIST WITHIN THE FIRM?

The partner and senior manager positions are not for everyone. Being stuck in senior manager limbo and feeling the pressure to successfully deliver across the client, team, and company can be physically and emotionally taxing. This is where many people face that career crossroads: Partner, independent consultant, entrepreneurship, or industry hire? Another option is specializing in-house for your firm in roles such as recruiting/training, business development, or operations.

Louisa Gantley is a mentor of mine who opted for the in-house route. When I discussed this decision with her, she was forthright in the trade-offs: "I missed the direct client interaction, the camaraderie that comes with working with a team to solve a problem, and that sense of satisfaction you get when you deliver a product to a client. Being in more of an operational role limited my interactions with other consultants and being a part of those teams." But while Louisa missed the intellectual horsepower of working across a team of very smart people to solve business problems and build relationships with a client, there were several factors that led her toward serving in operational roles for several firms:

> Being in these roles gave me a chance to build and test my entrepreneurial spirit without the risk of going out on my own. I was able to apply a number of the skills that I had developed as a consultant, work with very smart people to help focus on the bigger picture of building a practice, and be directly responsible for building a team. My current role has me doing recruiting and human resources, business development and building relationships, and strategy at the practice level. I would not have had these opportunities as a consultant.

Like many consultants who pivoted their careers or stepped off the partner track, Louisa also shared that her priorities had shifted to her family. Being in an internal role limited her travel and provided her with a steadier home life. While there was an allure to going independent and being your own boss, Louisa had seen a number of friends, colleagues, and teammates struggle with the feast-or-famine nature of independent consulting. An internal operations role provided her with the comfortable middle ground to flex those entrepreneurial muscles to build business strategy and hedge the risks of being independent.

FOCUS AND ITS DRAWBACKS

As Louisa's story shows, these coveted internal roles can enable consultants to (potentially) downshift to a better work-life balance and focus on a particular aspect of the firm. However, with any career decision, there are trade-offs to consider. For one, your career trajectory becomes more limited as your focus closes doors across other aspects of the firm. With your transition to an operationally focused, less billable role, you may see a decline in salary, bonuses, or other aspects of compensation. Depending on the role, you may also find less stability, as these roles are often the first to be cut when there is a downturn.

BETTER WORK-LIFE BALANCE

On the positive side, an internal role may provide a little more control and autonomy over your schedule. You are no longer needed to put out fires that inevitably pop up on your project team, with clients, or in leading proposal efforts. Your role becomes a bit more defined as you focus on a core aspect of the business. Firm service can be less demanding than client service, and your time is no longer the client's time. Many consultants choose this path because they do not see, or aspire to, Partner in the future or may want to focus more time on family.

Louisa's decision was also a function of timing. Serving as a federal business process improvement consultant, Louisa came across an opportunity to lead an R&D team for a professional services organization. The role specifically sought someone with financial, operational, and marketing expertise to build a new business line. Louisa approached the partner she worked for, who was a mentor of hers, and discussed the opportunity. The partner opined that it provided solid growth prospects – and that should this path lead to a dead-end, she would always be welcome back.

Louisa leveraged her consulting skills in the new role and thrived. During an economic downturn, she quickly found a role back in federal consulting. She took on additional responsibilities and led business development efforts in information technology and financial public-sector consulting. This provided Louisa with the chance to keep a foot in consulting, leverage her talents, and maintain a solid network of colleagues and mentors.

****

To successfully make this transition, assess your priorities and consider whether specialization and an operational career track is right for you. Evaluate the various career opportunities in-house, align your strengths, and begin building your knowledge and skill set by taking part in firm initiatives centered around that particular area. Get involved in recruiting and interviewing if you are passionate about growing the firm. Become more active in leading proposals and marketing your firm's value proposition if you are interested in business development. Lead operational initiatives that may feed into larger firm functions. There are endless paths and by building a bridge through firm initiatives, you can start aligning your knowledge and skills to potential openings. Just as Louisa did, maintain relationships and keep the doors open should you ever desire to return to consulting.

43

DO YOU WANT TO BE AN INDEPENDENT CONSULTANT?

Professionals are increasingly valuing flexibility, the ability to work for themselves, and greater autonomy and control. Becoming an independent consultant can often provide all of these benefits. Again, there are trade-offs to consider. A firm connotes a brand, stability, benefits, a network, and often a steady stream of clients. You'll have access to expertise and in-house tools and solutions. You may have departments explicitly focused on marketing, business development, recruiting, and training. There will be stability in knowing that your next project or two may already be on the books and that you may spend little time "on the bench." However, as we've learned, a firm has expectations around your time, performance targets, and contributions to the company. And managing a team, building business, and leading firm initiatives can be emotionally and physically draining. You may perform at a high level on all of these fronts and still not advance.

The decision to become an independent consultant is not an easy one but it is becoming increasingly common. Indeed, nearly 40% of Stanford's Graduate School of Business students[25] will serve as independent consultants at some stage in their career. People choose to become free agents (while also serving as their own agents) for a number of reasons: avoiding burnout, focus and expertise on a particular client, greater ownership of their schedule, and, for some, money. I've seen talented consultants leave their firms because they felt they could earn more money with a client that has expressed an interest in hiring them. I've also known people who went independent because they wanted more flexibility to set their hours and the freedom that comes with not having to endlessly march toward year-end metrics and performance reviews. Becoming an independent consultant can offer an alternative to the long hours and late nights. It can be liberating to know that you have a fixed project that will provide you a steady income stream and then live off of what you make for the rest of the year or spend time with family and friends before your next project. Many talented consultants also choose to go independent at the tail end of their careers, as they prepare for retirement and seek ways to wind down while also earning additional income.

Although independent consulting can occur at various stages and for all the reasons mentioned above, I find that most people go independent when they have a client that is already willing to hire just them – that they have a solid relationship that translates into business. You may have developed opportunities for this while in your firm. You've likely built some strong relationships with prospective clients who know your expertise and the value that you bring to their organization. You've also probably built strong networks in or across firms. Both of these serve as potential sales channels and an opportunity to build a client base. Marketing and business development will be handled by you, rather than a department, and your network will contribute to your net worth. You know your skills, relationships, and market value the best and should pursue roles based on these skills, the relationships that you have established, and the market need.

Being an independent consultant enables you to have greater flexibility and control of your time. There are no "mandatory optional" events to attend, business targets to meet, or performance evaluations to deliver. This can be very liberating, particularly for those who have slogged for years in the consulting grind. Your sole focus, once you have landed a client, is using your expertise to deliver excellent work. The job becomes simplified – you establish a client or clients (often already established before you go independent), set your value (which may be at the same rate, or even lower than what your firm billed you as), and put your skills into action to deliver stellar results.

Often, the best form of business development is retaining existing clients through your customer service, relationships, and impact. Many independent consultants have built comfortable careers serving on a range of short-term projects built through relationships, referrals, and hustling, or serving on longer-term projects as "in-house" consultants. They are able to bill based on their expertise and do not need to factor in as much for a profit margin, overhead costs, and other fixed or variable costs. This enables them to charge a market rate based on the value they bring, how they value their time, and what they are comfortable with. Since you are selling expertise, your costs are low and most of what you collect will go into your wallet.

****

Mike Thomas is one of those talented consultants who opted to give independent consulting a try. Mike had been a high-performing consultant at his firm for five years, working 60 or so hours a week, and was evaluating whether or not he wanted to make a push for partner. Mike and I commiserated over changing priorities, and as he considered starting a family, he knew that work-life balance and flexibility was going to become increasingly more important to him. Mike had a conversation with his firm as his project was starting to wind down. He had built a great relationship with his current client and was able to stay on with the client for about a four- to five-month period. While the stability of a firm, health coverage, and benefits of a 401(k) were lost, Mike earned substantially more on an hourly basis, was working considerably fewer hours (around 40 hours a week), and was able to obtain the work-life balance that he sought.

Independent consulting was not without its drawbacks. Mike had to pound the pavement to find his next client and ensure that the next check was coming in. He ultimately found another client that was seeking a presence where he was located and an understanding of the clients he served. This set him up for the next year and a half, during which time he could contemplate his next career move and decide whether independent consulting would be something he'd pursue long term.

****

Growth is the main challenge for independent consultants. You may enter the fray with a contract or two, but eventually those dry up. Time needs to be devoted to building a brand and portfolio and establishing your next client or clients. For many, this is the most frustrating piece of independent consulting. You left a firm to get away from business development, but becoming an independent consultant not only makes you a free agent, but also your own agent selling your skills and value. This takes time, and you are probably going to devote 10 to 15 hours a week until you've built a brand and established a solid book of business.

There is a very simple formula for independent consulting – you work, you get paid. You build business, you build stability. Independent consulting can be lucrative and offer greater flexibility and autonomy, but it also can be challenging. There is the challenge of not having a team, there is the challenge of not having the brand recognition of a firm, and there is the challenge of an unsteady income stream. It can be feast or famine, and you need to plan your vacations and budget around what is expected to come in and when you have gaps in projects. While independent consulting can be empowering, it can also be lonely serving in a consulting army of one, especially when you're on teams filled with consultants from other firms.

****

While the path of independent consulting can work for someone who loves networking and has built solid contacts and client relationships, is well-organized and adept at managing themselves, and has valuable real-world experience, it can be lonely, challenging to build a brand, and fraught with uncertainty over that next paycheck and future client. As freelancing becomes more common, independent consulting may become a more regular and viable option. Build your market presence, network, and client contacts to help set yourself up for the launch of a successful independent consulting career.

44

WHAT OPPORTUNITIES EXIST BEYOND CONSULTING?

Consulting builds readily transferable skills that will benefit you at any stage in your career and across diverse positions and industries. I have witnessed countless job opportunities across industries that have highlighted in their position descriptions a preference for a consulting background, because core consulting skills can be applied across a diverse range of roles. For many, particularly those who are not on the partner track, leaving consulting is a natural and welcome progression in their careers. Many consulting firms recognize this and have established alumni networks to broaden your network and expand your career opportunities. Common opportunities beyond independent consulting include (1) industry (in-house roles such as strategy), (2) entrepreneurship, and (3) social sector roles.

INDUSTRY HIRES

Companies like McKinsey, Boston Consulting Group, and Bain have extensive alumni networks that enable them to both extend their firm's brand and reputation and also leverage them for sales opportunities, employment, and industry insights. Sheryl Sandberg, Facebook's chief operating officer, is just one of many McKinsey alumni who have moved from consulting to the C-Suite. Industry roles are attractive because they often provide greater focus, balance, and the lens of one client – your company. These positions can be lucrative; the salary, stock options, and benefits that come with a leadership role at a successful company can far exceed those of a partner. Consulting provides a core skill set for stepping into management roles. Being able to think strategically, break objectives into executable actions, conduct qualitative and quantitative analysis, and influence and motivate teams make former consultants very attractive industry hires and position them for success in these roles.

****

For Andrew Synnott, it took two years at a high-performing firm to help him to realize that the work was not particularly fulfilling for him. A major reason for this was that the projects he supported were not scoped for execution. Often, he would help build a plan or deliver a recommendation and it would be the client, not his firm, that would carry this through and execute. As Andrew described it, "The satisfaction of leading an effort to fruition wasn't there. I'm not wired to take great satisfaction from delivering analysis and recommendations alone, no matter how robust, insightful, or intellectual. I like seeing it play out and create the impact we planned, and/ or leading and iterating the effort along the way."

When he was transitioned out of the firm, Andrew found that consulting had prepared him well for industry roles and that his communication skills and executive presence; structured, hypothesis-driven problem-solving; influencing and motivation leadership skills; tenacity and ability to adapt work pace; and client management skills all served him well in his next role in industry – where he was able to design, execute, implement, and directly see his efforts bear fruit.

When I pressed Andrew on the trade-offs or anything that he missed about consulting, he recounted, "The ongoing learning that comes with being surrounded by some of the best and brightest and the intellectual horsepower that you have access to in consulting is unmatched. It was invigorating to be in a room filled with people much smarter than me." Andrew made sure to highlight that there are very smart people in industry as well, and that some of the best moments in industry were getting to the whiteboard and problem-solving with a number of former consultants. He also shared that he missed the drive, tenacity, and fierce urgency of his consulting teammates. As a consultant, you are brought in to solve a very complex problem in a short period of time, and the focused intensity, the intellectual stimulation of problem-solving, and the camaraderie of doing the work in a diverse team are hard to match in industry. Moreover, Andrew highlighted the investment that many consulting firms make in training. There is an expectation that as you succeed, you will share lessons learned, best practices, and train others using leading-edge experiences, methods, and frameworks, while the sheer fact that you are surrounded by so much intellectual stimulation enables you to stretch, grow, and learn.

Andrew shared five primary benefits of working in industry. First and foremost, he felt that he had much greater control over his time. As a consultant, traveling to client sites enabled him to compartmentalize, but even when he was on local projects, he felt that he was "here, but not." This was inherent in the pace and complexity of the project, and while many consulting firms – his former firm included – provide pulse-checks and have implemented systems to manage burnout, these systems don't always correct for the pressure that consultants feel to perform. The second advantage, Andrew noted, was that industry focuses much less on micro-performance. In consulting, your drive to constantly improve leads to almost continual feedback on how you led a particular meeting, how you managed someone's performance, and the impact of each slide on a presentation. While this does lead to hyper-growth, Andrew found that industry often enabled more time to focus on effectiveness over an extended period of time. A third benefit is the diversity of teams that you work with in industry. Of course, consulting teams can be diverse, with expertise across multifunctional skill sets. However, consultants are hired with particular skill sets in mind – analytics, structured, hypothesis-driven thinking, critical thinking – and teams are composed of people leveraging these skills. In industry, you may need to work across operations, marketing, and more functions and dynamics to solve complex challenges. This diversity of expertise provides its own form of learning and enables you to tap into particular functions to solve a business problem. Fourth, in industry, projects are seen beyond just recommendations. This was an aspect that Andrew particularly enjoyed and one reason he chose to leave consulting. At the risk of oversimplifying, consultants come in to solve a problem, conduct analysis, make a recommendation and then the client either often hires a different team to execute or does the execution themselves. In contrast, because you have a more clearly defined role and responsibility in industry, you are often part of the design, delivery, and execution of a project. This can be more meaningful and gratifying as you own the recommendations and get to see the impact and experience results firsthand over time. Fifth, Andrew mentioned industry's more clearly defined performance metrics. Metrics and outputs may unroll over the course of the efforts that you are leading and with this comes greater autonomy to manage your schedule to meet these measures.

While industry roles will undoubtedly vary, the bottom line is that as a former consultant you already are branded with established credentials. Hiring managers expect you to come in as a high performer with the training, intellectual horsepower, adaptability, toolkit, and drive to thrive in the role. And more often than not, you will.

ENTREPRENEURSHIP

Consultants' ability to think creatively, evaluate opportunities, and conduct benchmarking analysis and market research can draw many to entrepreneurship. Whether founding their own startup or joining a fledgling venture, consultants can draw from their toolkit, industry understanding, and past projects to help startups build their strategy and execute. Consultants see patterns emerge in businesses or have talked through the future of industries with a number of very smart businesspeople. They can use these skills at any phase of the startup, from ideation through development, launch, and growth. The list of consultants-turned-entrepreneurs is growing and includes such founders as Gagan Biyani of Udemy, Kathryn Minshew of the Muse (originally the Daily Muse), and serial entrepreneur Francesco Caio.

****

After over five years at McKinsey, Rohit Agarwal ventured into entrepreneurship. After trying his hand at entrepreneurship – launching a venture and learning a lot in the process – he joined Kiva, a microfinance nonprofit that extends loans to entrepreneurs, as Head of the United States. Rohit recounted the decision behind this pivot:

> The decision to leave McKinsey was twofold. One, we had a daughter and it was really challenging to get back on a plane and leave my family. I was enjoying the people, the topics, and was on a project that I loved, but life factored in. It became a family decision. Two, you are always in client services, and you are always at the behest of your client. I wanted more decision-making and autonomy. I first left to become an entrepreneur and applied my consulting experiences. I thought I'd be effective running a company, and I would be able to apply what I liked and did not like from various managers and executives that I learned from through my consulting projects. So much of my current role at Kiva, where I am essentially a general manager, is influencing and motivating. This is very much from consulting. I also say the most important thing is how you are motivating your team – and teaching,

actually, was even more important in developing this skill than consulting.

Rohit continues to have an eye toward entrepreneurship while gaining greater industry insights and impacting countless entrepreneurs through his role at Kiva.

SOCIAL SECTOR

Many consultants recognize that with great skills and advantages come great responsibility to their communities and society and choose to use their consulting powers for the public good. A number of them have transitioned into social-sector roles to help maximize impact, solve complex societal challenges, and better the lives of those around them. They are able to align organizations for collective impact, communicate and market the need for funds to support their effort, and break the complex down into simple messages. Many former consultants have found homes in government, nonprofit, and higher education. Examples include David Coleman, CEO of the College Board, Bernard Ferrari, dean emeritus of the Johns Hopkins Carey School of Business, and Pete Buttigieg, politician and former presidential candidate.

****

From going in-house for a company, to launching your own company, to incorporating yourself and consulting independently, consulting provides adaptable knowledge, skills, and networks that can be applied across industries, organizations, and opportunities. In each of these anecdotes, we've seen consultants learn from their experiences, leave with a stronger network, and have established credentials that make them attractive candidates across multiple diverse industries and roles.

45

HOW CAN YOU PIVOT YOUR CONSULTING CAREER?

As a sociology major in college, Maxine Teller got her first taste of consulting interning for a strategic innovation boutique firm, at which she then worked full-time after graduation. The exposure to a variety of industries and client challenges not only gave her a great breadth of experience early in her career, it also equipped her with an invaluable skill set that she'd later rely on. Maxine left her first job to deepen her business knowledge by earning her MBA. After graduation, she cofounded a startup and then worked as director of strategy and business development at Washingtonpost Newsweek Interactive. Maxine was laid off three months after returning from maternity leave with her first child. Balancing her growing family and the need to make a living, Maxine forayed into independent consulting, working on a contract basis and leveraging her strategy expertise on a project in an industry that was new to her. This project illuminated four things for Maxine: (1) As a mom, "flexibility was everything." (2) She wasn't interested in navigating the internal politics to climb the corporate ladder—what she valued most was "independence." (3) Consultants, particularly those who position themselves as trusted advisors to senior executives, can have tremendous influence – and sometimes, greater impact – on the direction of the organization than employees sometimes can. (4) Consulting provides never-ending learning opportunities in new organizations and industries.

Maxine would go on to launch her own business strategy consulting firm, Maximize, and over the past 17 years, has worked with C-level executives at 30-plus corporations, federal agencies, and nonprofits. Consulting has afforded her the opportunity to use her business strategy, innovation, and digital transformation expertise to improve her client organizations' efficiency and effectiveness. By fortunate happenstance, Maxine was able to turn a layoff into an opportunity and establish her niche. Maxine emphasizes,

"Data is the competitive currency. However, too many organizations don't know how to access, analyze, or use data to strategically run their businesses." She credits her early experience in consulting for propelling her into starting her firm. While this was not her original plan, it is one that has served her and her family well. Maxine explains that in this industry, it can be "feast or famine" and having a partner with health insurance and a more stable income helps steady the inevitable dry spells of consulting. Maxine has used consulting as a tool to craft her career. While she had opportunities at larger firms, she's preferred directly advising executives while having the flexibility of being her own boss. Her story is one of many highlighting the versatility of consulting and the opportunities consultants have to shape their own – and their clients' – destiny.

****

As Maxine Teller' story shows, career pivots can occur by happenstance. More often, these pivots are intentional shifts with a set purpose in mind. Ideally, your pivot from consulting is methodical, deliberate, and maybe even a little uncomfortable. Fortunately, as a consultant, you are primed for building a plan, thriving in ambiguity, and taking meaningful steps towards results. You may be looking to pivot for a number of reasons – you've plateaued, you feel disengaged, you no longer feel challenged or no longer enjoy what you do, you want greater pay or work-life balance. Before planning your pivot, start by (here it goes) *crafting your consulting career*. Figure out the root cause of your dissatisfaction and assess whether you can request, build a business case for, or initiate changes to lead you out of the doldrums at your current firm. If you are unable to do so with your current role, prioritize what factors are most important for you in your next role, take an inventory of the skills you have, and identify your gaps. As a consultant, you have developed many transferable skills that will be valued in many roles.

Once you've identified your gaps, start building your resume to address them (yes, you can even go back to chapter 3, "How Do You Build Your Consulting Resume?"). This might involve rephrasing your resume to showcase certain common skills between consulting and your ideal role, reaching out to your extensive network to better understand what it takes to succeed in your target profession, and determining the time and cost you need in order to fill these gaps. And – as you are now well-versed in – benchmark yourself against other industry professionals in that role and set targets to help you better meet those standards. This could be talking to a certain number of people in that profession a week, or crafting thought leadership articles around a particular topic, or devoting time to building knowledge or a skill.

****

Mike Thomas, the consultant who went independent (chapter 43), ultimately shifted his approach. After the birth of his daughter, Mike wanted something a bit more stable and that provided greater work-life balance than consulting. Independent consulting had provided flexibility, control, and a higher salary, but Mike also foresaw those "feast or famine" periods. Looking to pivot his career, Mike aligned his core consulting skills – strategy, communication, analytics – to a role with a financial services company and was ultimately hired. This pivot, like any, came with trade-offs. Mike had the work-life balance and stability that he prioritized, but took a bit of a salary decline from consulting. In all, he is probably coming out ahead hourly, and you cannot put a price on a steady paycheck. He's thriving in his new role, has peace of mind, and is able to spend more time with his family – all pivot wins!

****

An essential part of any career pivot is your pitch. Practice this until you have fully convinced yourself that this is the right move. Tell a cohesive story of what skills you developed in consulting, how they apply to your target profession, why you are making that transition, and why that transition is the right move now. Once you have convinced yourself, try to convince others. Depending on how your firm views pivots, whether this is a welcome addition to the alumni network or whether you will be placed in the persona non grata hall of shame, begin to signal your intentions through LinkedIn, updating your resume, and tapping into resources (your firm's alumni network if an option). The beauty of a pivot is that you can effortlessly return to your starting point or use your new positioning to further pivot to another location.

While I ultimately stayed in consulting, I recently pivoted from more of a strategy and operations role to more of a technology consulting and change management focused role. Before making the move, I had attempted to craft my job at my current firm by sharing my desire to take on added responsibility in business development, operations, and practice strategy. We could not reach a compromise on the time dedicated to client delivery and firm growth, so, starting to feel pigeonholed, I began to consider alternatives.

Prior to joining my current team, most of my work focused on process improvements and aligning actions to strategic initiatives. I had limited experience in digital transformation and cloud services. Recognizing that these were gaps I had to overcome, I made sure to emphasize my background designing strategic communications, facilitating sessions, and developing and implementing plans for organizational change. These experiences all aligned exceedingly well with change management and helped build a bridge to what I would be doing on the technology implementation side. To further address my gaps, I highlighted certifications that were applicable to the role and began proactively taking training to strengthen my knowledge of digital transformation efforts. During my interview, I highlighted one of my values of continuous learning and improvement and that while I was thriving in my current (now former) role, this new role would present an opportunity for me to apply my skills in a fundamentally different way, provide a different perspective for the team, and learn in a vibrant technology ecosystem.

Currently, I'm evaluating a partial pivot to higher education as a professor of practice, teaching business courses to the next generation of business leaders, consultants, and entrepreneurs. I entered with a number of assumptions that were quickly dashed by professors, deans, and those with far more higher education experience than me (basically anyone in higher education). This caused me to shift my approach and focus greater time on writing, thought leadership, and sharing lessons learned. In fact, my desire to mentor, coach, and learn from others and the advice I received influenced me to write this book.

I hope you have gained from my own partial pivot – the conversations I have had, mistakes I have made, and the lessons that I have learned and am sharing with you – and that you will share with others.

CONCLUSION

You might be a consultant if…

- You gratuitously turn phrases into acronyms (PPS, PBA, IIF, EEF, LAC).
- You have a penchant for writing 10-page reports with six people you don't know.
- Every problem or challenge is viewed as an "opportunity for improvement."
- You can spell "paradigm" and you actually know what a paradigm is.
- You cannot help but use words and phrases like "synergy," "leverage," "integration," "core competencies," and "network effect" in any conversation, even those with your one-year old daughter.

Consulting is more than a profession – it is a lifestyle. Within a year of launching my consulting career, I noticed that my vernacular had changed, my approach to problem-solving had changed, and I consistently sought more growth, leadership, and "opportunities for improvement." Everything became a process improvement project. This lifestyle is not for everyone, and as your priorities change, there is a very real chance that you may need to adapt as well. The beauty of consulting is that it opens doors while also leaving the light on for you.

This compilation of experience, anecdotes, and lessons would have saved me a great deal of time and effort and led me to different decisions and conclusions, throughout my career. It is not just the partners at nine figure–plus practices who have lessons to share. Countless consultants have made career decisions based on what they value, and the title and salary that you seek at the beginning of your career may be traded in for work-life balance, flexibility, or other priorities at a different stage. Ultimately, you define your version of success, and knowing the crossroads can help you to better map out your journey.

I hope this book helps you to more effectively navigate your career, anticipate those critical decisions, and make the choices that are best for you. I hope it provides you with an opportunity to plan, reflect, and grow. Perhaps, most importantly, I hope that as you succeed in your career, you capture your own lessons learned and help others use these lessons to be successful. Good luck crafting your consulting career!

RECOMMENDED READING

A book on how to craft your consulting career would not be complete without a list of resources to help you develop and enhance your skills. As a PPS and lifelong learner, you should prioritize and dedicate time to reading, writing or presenting, and honing your craft. Each of these books is carefully curated from my own library and comes highly recommended by many other consultants.

As someone who has committed to reading 50-plus business, management, and professional development books a year, I've seen my library grow substantially over time. My reading list also continues to grow as I continue to ask my PBA, consultants, and network for reading recommendations. The tailored list I've presented here comprises the 25+ books that have been the most influential in my career, broken into my top five recommended books across five core categories: (1) Consulting Preparation, (2) Communications, (3) Customer Service, (4) Essential Consulting, and (5) Management/ Leadership. Each section is prioritized to help you focus your time on crafting your consulting career.

Commit to reading these books over the next six months (a book a week) or as your schedule allows to help the seeds of knowledge gained from this book to germinate. You may opt to start with the top pick in each category before moving onto the rest, or you may opt to focus on a critical development area and read all of the books in that category before moving on to another. Either way, make that investment in lifelong learning and share, recommend, and add your own books to these lists (and feel free to reach out to me with your suggestions).

CONSULTING PREPARATION

These books will probably apply most to readers who are in the stage of learning about consulting and planning or launching their consulting careers. That being said, it never hurts for more seasoned consultants to brush up on their skills, learn what aspiring consultants are reading, and reflect on the takeaways from these books. Doing this could help those more seasoned consultants to become better recruiters and mentors, and to reflect on their consulting preparation.

1. *Case In Point: Complete Case Interview Preparation, 11th edition*, by Marc Cosentino (Burgee Press, 2020)[26]	The "MBA Bible" – this book provides interview tips, case interview preparation, and insights from case interview guru Marc Cosentino.
1a. *Case In Point: Government and Nonprofit*, by Marc Cosentino and Evan Piekara (Burgee Press, 2019)[27]	OK – I know that I cheated a little bit by opening this section with a 1a. This book is a letter to my younger self of what I wish I knew about social-sector consulting. If you are interested in government, nonprofit, corporate social responsibility, or the social sector, then this book provides more focused industry insights.
2. *The MECE Muse: 100+ Selected Practices, Unwritten Rules, and Habits of Great Consultants*, by Christie Lindor (SDP Publishing, 2018)[28]	This book is packed with insider tips, best practices, and teachings from a seasoned consultant and provides takeaways from interviews with many successful consultants.
3. *Good to Great: Why Some Companies Make the Leap ... And Others Don't*, by Jim Collins, (HarperCollins, 2001)[29]	A classic, and one of the most influential business books of all time. This book concisely shares key takeaways and principles from a comprehensive study on business success. Its central theme is that organizations make conscious and disciplined decisions that lead to greatness (or lose focus and discipline, leading to their decline). The principles in this book provide understanding that can be leveraged across projects, teams, and organizations.
4. *The McKinsey Way: Using the Techniques of Top Strategic Consultants to Help You and Your Business*, by Ethan Rasiel (McGraw-Hill, 1999)[30]	This book provides perspective on how top consultants solve problems and shares methodologies and frameworks for tackling complex challenges.

5. *Strategy Maps: Converting Intangible Assets into Tangible Outcomes*, by Robert Kaplan and David Norton (Harvard Business School Publishing, 2004)[31]	This book provides a blueprint for organizations to build strategy that aligns processes, people, and information technology for superior performance.

COMMUNICATIONS

Successful consultants are effective communicators. I've found that while technical skill and competencies may help you advance in the earlier stages of your consulting career, those who progress and are promoted faster and who are more successful in the later stages of their careers are strong communicators. As you advance, your ability to persuade, influence and motivate, present, coach and provide feedback, and sell become more important. These have been the most influential books in helping me to develop communications skills.

1. *Influence: The Psychology of Persuasion*, by Robert Cialdini (Harper Business, 2006)[32]	This groundbreaking book provides a wealth of knowledge on emotional intelligence and human behavior. Use this book to influence others and strengthen communications. Better understanding Cialdini's six principles – (1) reciprocity, (2) scarcity, (3) authority, (4) consistency, (5) liking, and (6) consensus – will make you a much more effective consultant.
2. *Made to Stick: Why Some Ideas Take Hold and Others Come Unstuck*, by Chip and Dan Heath (Random House, 2008)[33]	This is undoubtedly one of the books that most influenced my career. It provides case studies and tools to guide communications practices you can use to make an idea stand out. I use their SUCCESS (simple, unexpected, concrete, credible, emotional, stories) model as a checklist whenever presenting an idea and try to infuse concepts into those presentations.

3. *Getting to Yes: Negotiating an Agreement Without Giving In*, by Roger Fisher and William Ury (Penguin, 2011)[34]	This book shares best practices for approaching negotiations and aligning communications to reach an agreement.
4. *Never Split the Difference: Negotiating As If Your Life Depended on It*, by Chris Voss (HarperCollins, 2016)[35]	This book provides nine effective tactics and strategies to improve persuasion and communication from a former hostage negotiator.
5. *Case In Point: Case Competitions: Creating Winning Strategy Presentations for Case Competitions and Job Offers*, by Marc Cosentino, Kara Cupoli, and Jason Rife (Burgee Press, 2017)[36]	This book shares how to build teamwork, presentation, and analytical skills in diagnosing a problem and providing recommendations. While the focus is case competitions, the practices are beneficial well beyond them.

CUSTOMER SERVICE

Consulting is a customer-centric business where you win work, retain clients, and build a portfolio through your ability to sell, deliver, and exceed the expectations of your client. Each of these books provides insights on how you gain trust, build relationships, and deliver exceptional client service.

1. *The Trusted Advisor*, by David Maister, Charles Green, and Robert Galford (Touchstone, 2001)[37]	A classic on how to build trust, position yourself as an advisor, and provide essential services to the client.
2. *How to Win Friends and Influence People*, by Dale Carnegie (Pocket Books, 1998)[38]	Another classic on building relationships, gaining influence, and persuading others.

3. *It Starts with Clients: Your 100 Day Plan to Build Lasting Relationships*, Andrew Sobel (Wiley, 2020)[39]	Building lasting relationships is about building connections, understanding needs, and adding value. This book provides anecdotes, guiding questions, and insights to help you provide better service.
4. *Ask Powerful Questions: Create Conversations That Matter*, by Will Wise (CreateSpace, 2017)[40]	This book provides tools and a framework to ask questions, unlock insights, enhance understanding, and create stronger connections.
5. *Your Customer Rules Delivering the Me2B Experiences That Today's Customers Demand*, by Bill Price and David Jaffe (Jossey-Bass, 2014)[41]	Every interaction with the customer is critical, and with customers increasingly having access to more information, the balance of power has shifted. This book provides insights to improve those customer interactions.

ESSENTIAL CONSULTING

Project management, creative thinking, learning and drawing analogies, molding and modifying frameworks, analyzing, and interpreting and evaluating data all are core skills of consultants. Each of these books provide frameworks, tools, and understanding that can drive you to become a greater consultant.

1. *Getting Things Done: The Art of Stress-Free Productivity*, by David Allen (Penguin, 2015)[42]	Managing your projects and life with ease and elegance will increase productivity, make you a more desirable teammate, and enable you to more successfully contribute to projects. This book provides tools, frameworks, and guidance for prioritizing and managing your time.
2. *Six Thinking Hats*, by Edward de Bono (Back Bay Books, 1999)[43]	A unique and practical guide on thinking and how to leverage six viewpoints to improve decision-making. The ideas in this book can be particularly effective in helping teams compromise, see blind spots, or plan and prepare for critical issues.

3. *Mindset: The New Psychology of Success*, by Carol Dweck (Penguin Random House, 2007)[44]	This book provides insights into establishing a growth mindset and enhancing your abilities. Being a constant learner and instilling these principles will help make you more effective in whichever career that you choose.
4. *The Balanced Scorecard: Translating Strategy into Action*, by Robert Kaplan and David Norton (Harvard Business Review Press, 1996)[45]	This book provides guidance on how to translate a company's vision and strategy into action using a focused format and framework for increasing performance.
5. *Competing on Analytics: The New Science of Winning*, by Thomas Davenport and Jeanne Harris (Harvard Business Review Press, 2017)[46]	Organizations are building competitive advantages around data, and this book provides tools and studies to show how organizations are using data to drive performance.

MANAGEMENT/ LEADERSHIP

Consultants need to apply effective management and leadership skills to accomplish tasks and address challenges and opportunities. Management often revolves around controlling a group and helping them execute to accomplish a goal. Leadership is often associated with the individual's ability to influence, motivate, and empower people to contribute to organizational success. Together, the two are a powerful combination. These books provide critical insights into how to build influence, lead, and manage a group toward changes or a goal.

1. *Leading Change: Why Transformation Efforts Fail*, by John Kotter (Harvard Business Review Press, 2012)[47]	In essence, every project that you encounter will have some element of change management and will be fundamentally about helping a client change. John Kotter's timeless book provides an eight-step framework for managing change as well as stories, case studies, and best practices – and why transformation efforts don't always work.
2. *ADKAR: A Model for Change in Business, Government, and Our Community*, by Jeffrey Hiatt (Prosci, Inc., 2006)[48]	This book provides a holistic, scalable, and customizable model for observing and influencing change.
3. *The 7 Habits of Highly Effective People*, by Stephen Covey (Free Press, 2004)[49]	A classic and principled approach for developing leadership skills that enable you to address and solve problems.
4. *Grit: The Power of Passion and Perseverance*, by Angela Duckworth (Scribner, 2016)[50]	This book explores the psychology behind developing perseverance that enables you to succeed and perform at a higher level. Undoubtedly, you will need to grow, learn, and will face challenges as a consultant and this book will help you and your teams overcome those obstacles.
5. *Radical Candor: Be a Kick-Ass Boss Without Losing Your Humanity*, by Kim Scott (St. Martin's Press, 2019)[51]	This book shares tools and a framework for creating a culture of compassion, a cohesive team, and collaboratively achieving results.

Lifelong learning is not just a best practice for consulting, it is a practice for your personal and professional life. Make learning and continuous improvement part of what distinguishes you, enables you to evolve and adapt, and be part of your individual competitive advantage. The wisdom stored in the approximately 7,500 pages listed above will provide you with the tools, acumen, and knowledge to unlock higher performance and potential in your career. Happy learning!

ABOUT THE AUTHOR

Evan Piekara is the coauthor of *Case In Point: Government and Nonprofit* with Marc Cosentino. He has nearly 15 years of experience working in consulting, education, and the nonprofit sector. Evan launched his career as a member of Teach For America (TFA), teaching sixth- and seventh-grade English and history in the South Bronx. During this time, he served as a teacher, volunteer, and in operational support and training roles for the organization. After joining BDO, Evan supported the company's launch of their Public Sector management consulting practice and led strategy, operations, human capital, and technology engagements. At BDO, Evan also led internal efforts around methodology development, practice development, business development, and recruiting. Evan currently serves as a Senior Manager in Acumen Solutions' Change Management Practice (Acumen has been acquired by Salesforce), where he supports digital transformation and organizational change efforts for government, nonprofit, and private-sector clients.

Evan holds a range of professional certifications in change management, project management, technology, conflict resolution, process improvement, and total quality management. He has presented on a number of topics, including change management, conflict resolution, and performance measurement and evaluation; and he delivers workshops globally to aspiring consultants. He has served in leadership roles on nonprofit boards and leveraged consulting experience to help these boards address complex challenges.

Evan is passionate about mentoring, coaching, and helping others achieve career success. He also believes in the power of continuous improvement, capturing lessons learned, and sharing these lessons to help others navigate their own unique career paths.

Evan earned an MBA from Georgetown's McDonough School of Business, a master's in the Science of Teaching from Pace University, and a bachelor's in Government and Economics from Connecticut College.

ACKNOWLEDGMENTS

Writing a book is a practice in perseverance, and it truly takes a village to produce such a work. I'd like to start by thanking my wife, Prita Piekara, who provided time, constant encouragement, and feedback as I thought through these concepts, and my daughter, Anaiya Piekara, for the smiles that helped me recharge during those writing breaks. Thank you to Dottie Hartsfield for being the guardian angel for our family. Thank you to all of my friends and family in Belchertown, Massachusetts, for your support.

I'd like to also thank Marc Cosentino for serving as a pioneer in the consulting preparation space and for providing a platform for us to share ideas, best practices, and insights with countless current and aspiring consultants, recruiters, and career counselors. I've personally learned a lot from his books, workshops, and partnership and have gained so much from working with him. I'd also like to thank Monica Jainschigg for her careful review, thoughtful edits, and feedback – her insights and expertise have led to a significantly improved book! Thank you to Jayme Johnson for your design insights, expertise, and attention to detail. Thank you to the reviewers Christie Lindor, Dolph Goldenburg, Doreen Amorosa, Eric Williamson, Joe Stimac, Matthew Chambers, Prerika Agarwal, and Smarthveer Sidana for their feedback and endorsement!

Being a lifelong learner means prioritizing mentoring others, being mentored, and learning from colleagues. I wrote this book to capture insights that I've learned and shared through hundreds of informational interviews (from both sides of the table). I cannot thank each of these people enough for sharing their insights, thoughts, and expertise with our readers and me! Thank you (in order of appearance): Shelley Rappaport, Rohit Agarwal, Yashomati Bachul Koul, Andrew Synnott, Prer Bania, Tiffany Yang, Eric

Williamson, Helen Walker, Dave Brant, Cassandra Isbell, Jim Riddick, Mike Thomas (pseudonym), Maxine Teller, Louisa Gantley, and the countless others who anonymously lent their stories, anecdotes, and insights to this book. Each of these people are leaders, mentors, and experts in their own right and have graciously shared their time with me and were willing to connect with others on LinkedIn.

Many of the people mentioned above have served on my personal board of advisors. I'd also like to thank the following people for being on my PBA during various stages of my career: Leo Higdon, Nancy Mistretta, Armando Bengochea, Dorothy James, Kendall Doble, Harris Rosenheim, Leidy Valencia-Severson, Grant Hogan, Ken Kabel, Jamie Glanton Costello, Dra. Lois Mendez-Catlin, Annie Scott, Tori McKenna, Isaac "Chip" Clothier, Cheryl Banker, Ivan Tatis, Victoria Elenowitz, Lore Rasch, Karen Goldstein, Brad Allen, Felix Li, Elizabeth Spector Louden, Eugene Lee, John Harlow, Matt Dover, Bobby Adelson, Michelle Kim, Bill Novelli, Lawrence Verbiest, Brian Craigie, Idy Auner, Chuck Wolverton, Ricci Mulligan, Rick Swengros, Michelle Bryan, Nasir Qadree, the chain (you know who you are), Wanda Steptoe and to anyone who I may have missed from this list and the one above (as I mentioned, it takes a village). I've learned so much from each of you and appreciate your time, mentorship, and support.

I'd also like to thank the organizations that have helped me to grow, learn, and shape my experiences – Connecticut College, Teach For America, Pace University, the New Leaders Council, LeadIn (with a special thanks to founder Zarko Palankov and LeadIn fellows Anjana Sreedhar, Berenike Schriewer, Heather Ingram, and Phim Her), Georgetown McDonough School of Business, BDO Public Sector, Acumen Solutions, and Salesforce.

As I've highlighted throughout this book, board service provides a valuable opportunity to use your time and talents to better support the community and causes that are important to you. While I wish I had more time to give, I'd like to thank these organizations for providing me with the opportunity to serve, learn, and connect: Connecticut College Alumni Board of Directors and the Connecticut College Board of Trustees, New Endeavors by Women (NEW), DC Scholars Public Charter School Board of Trustees, and the Ward 5 Education Trust.

Finally, I'd like to thank my readers and followers on medium (evan.piekara), twitter (@evan_piekara), and those who read the casequestions.com blog.

Thank you to those current and future consultants who have reached out both through a shared network or on LinkedIn to ask those critical questions to help shape your careers.

Please share this information, refine it through your personal lens, and improve it so that others can benefit. Thank you.

ENDNOTES

1 (https://www.mbacrystalball.com/blog/2018/08/08/teacher-mba-management-consultant-career-change/)

2 https://hbr.org/2003/10/nice-girls-dont-ask

3 https://info.blackswanltd.com/never-split-the-difference

4 https://www.williamury.com/books/getting-to-yes/

5 https://www.nytimes.com/2019/12/03/us/mckinsey-ICE-immigration.html

6 https://popular.info/p/inside-deloittes-secret-contracts

7 https://hbr.org/2005/03/want-collaboration-accept-and-actively-manage-conflict

8 https://www.merriam-webster.com/dictionary/conflict

9 https://www.amazon.com/How-Work-Jerks-Getting-People/dp/0999456695

10 https://news.gallup.com/businessjournal/162953/tackle-employees-stagnating-engagement.aspx

11 https://hbr.org/2016/03/learning-to-learn

12 https://www.penguinrandomhouse.com/books/44330/mindset-by-carol-s-dweck-phd/

13   https://angeladuckworth.com/grit-book/

14   https://hbr.org/2018/05/the-right-way-to-respond-to-negative-feedback

15   https://www.radicalcandor.com/the-book/

16   https://www.franklincovey.com/the-7-habits/

17   https://hbr.org/2019/02/how-to-figure-out-how-much-influence-you-have-at-work?utm_source=twitter&utm_medium=social&utm_campaign=hbr)

18   https://hbr.org/2003/06/lets-hear-it-for-b-players

19   https://hbr.org/2019/03/the-feedback-fallacy

20   https://www.radicalcandor.com/

21   https://trustedadvisor.com/books/the-trusted-advisor

22   https://ssir.org/articles/entry/burnout_from_an_organizational_perspective

23   https://news.gallup.com/businessjournal/106912/turning-around-your-turnover-problem.aspx

24   https://ssir.org/articles/entry/burnout_from_an_organizational_perspective

25   https://www.gsb.stanford.edu/insights/should-you-become-independent-consultant

26   https://casequestions.com/about-us/

27   https://publicsectorcaseinterviewprep.com/author/evan-piekaragmail-com/

28   https://www.mecemuse.us/

29   https://www.jimcollins.com/books.html

30   https://managementconsulted.com/the-mckinsey-way-book-review/

31   https://store.hbr.org/product/strategy-maps-converting-intangible-assets-into-tangible-outcomes/1342

32   https://www.influenceatwork.com/

33   https://heathbrothers.com/books/made-to-stick/

34   https://www.williamury.com/books/getting-to-yes/

35   https://info.blackswanltd.com/never-split-the-difference

36   https://casequestions.com/books-and-web-based-training

37   https://davidmaister.com/books/ta/

38   https://www.amazon.com/How-Win-Friends-Influence-People/dp/0671027034

39   https://andrewsobel.com/it-starts-with-clients/

40   https://andrewsobel.com/it-starts-with-clients/

41   https://www.amazon.com/Your-Customer-Rules-Delivering-Experiences/dp/1118954777

42   https://gettingthingsdone.com/getting-things-done-the-art-of-stress-free-productivity/

43   https://www.amazon.com/Six-Thinking-Hats-Edward-Bono/dp/0316178314

44   https://www.penguinrandomhouse.com/books/44330/mindset-by-carol-s-dweck-phd/

45   https://store.hbr.org/product/the-balanced-scorecard-translating-

strategy-into-action/6513

46   https://www.tomdavenport.com/books/

47   https://www.kotterinc.com/book/leading-change/

48   https://store.prosci.com/bookstore/books.html

49   https://www.franklincovey.com/the-7-habits/

50   https://angeladuckworth.com/grit-book/

51   https://www.radicalcandor.com/the-book/

Made in the USA
Las Vegas, NV
13 July 2021